I0003211

Tech Tactics

Publishing and
Production Secrets

by William Keeley

Tech Tactics – Publishing and
Production Secrets
First Edition

Copyright © 2012
William Keeley
All Rights Reserved

ISBN-10: 1475214081
ISBN-13: 978-1475214086

Kindle Edition ASIN:B0087Z9EZW
Nook Edition BNID: 2940014743068

Table of Contents

Amazon, Create Space, and Kindle are Trademarks of Amazon, inc. iMovie, iPad, iPhone, and iPad are registered trademarks of Apple Computer, inc.

Windows, Windows XP, Windows Vista, Windows 7, Windows Movie Maker, and Windows Live Movie Maker, are registered trademarks of Microsoft Corporation.

All other trademarks not mentioned are registered trademarks of their respective companies.

This book is dedicated to Daniel Robert Keeley, "Beetle," my brother, the peacemaker.

Live to ride.   Ride to Live.

September 5, 1963 - January 24, 2011

Rest in Peace.

Introduction

This book, like the other books in William Keeley's Tech Tactics series is meant to provide information on how to accomplish a task with very little or no startup costs. In this case, this book talks about how to produce and publish various media from books and newsletters to quality CD's and DVD's. This book not only discusses the equipment needed but also free software that can accomplish the task at hand. The free software discussed in this book comes without strings attached, without spy ware, and without ad-ware unless otherwise spelled out. Many of the programs listed in this book will be compatible with industry standard, expensive programs that are commercially available. It is not the intent of the author to disparage the commercial products that are used as a matter of industry standard. However, in most cases, it is unnecessary to spend large amounts of money on such products if they are to be used only one time.

It is also very difficult for many people to come up with the money to buy these products in the first place. Using free equivalents allows people to work and produce revenue that can be used to buy the commercial products at a later time if these products are still desired.

While there are many tools out there for the Windows operating system that are discussed in this book, many of the better ones run in Linux, BSD, or Mac OSX, or any other derivative or clone of Unix. This is due to the fact that Linux and Windows developers generally come from two different schools of thought. Windows developers generally think about how they are going to make money from the software that they write. In other words, they code for cash. Much of Windows code, even though it is free to use remains closed source. This is sometimes due to the fear of violating third party licensing agreements, etc. Sometimes it is done just for the purpose of control.

Linux developers generally think about how they can make the software they write more useful or how to perform a task better. They write code in the hope that it will be useful for them and due to the GNU Public License, any code that is produced and distributed must include the source so that others can improve upon it. The GNU Public License is not a license meant to restrict or discourage the development of useful programs and other intellectual property. It is meant to encourage the development of useful programs and intellectual property. In other words, the GNU Public License has done for software innovation what traditional copyrights were supposed to do but now discourage.

This book is not about converting people to use Linux, but this short paragraph will mention ways of trying it. Most people who try it and use it for a month or two end up staying with it and not going back to Windows. One does not have to wipe his or her hard drive to try Linux. There are many other ways of trying it.

One, different versions or distributions of Linux can be downloaded as live CD's or boot CD's. Computers can boot up from these CD's, and Linux can be run without having to install it on the hard drive.

Two, a virtual machine such as Virtual Box (http://www.virtualbox.org) can be installed on Windows, and Linux can be installed within Virtual Box. For those who have relatively recently made machines or relatively updated machines should try this option. Some versions or distributions of Linux may not be configured to work on some hardware, but one should try several before distributions giving up. With the thousands upon thousands of free software applications with no strings attached, Linux is a great bargain for those who want to get away from the pay, pay merry-go-round. Much of the software is exactly what is needed for an outstanding publishing and production platform.

Is it possible for some twenty-something living in his parent's basement to become a published author, music producer, or movie director? Is it possible for that twenty-something to do it with just a computer, camcorder or even a camera phone? The answer to these questions is, "Yes." Inexpensive computers and electronic gadgets combined with the power of the Internet has finally given the establishment book and magazine publishers as well as music and movie moguls some real competition.

Individuals, as well as small outfits, can now make media that competes directly with establishment fare. In the Information Age, one can go as far as his or her talent and marketing skills will allow. Gone are the months of frustration of receiving rejection letters or no response at all from companies to which scripts, manuscripts, or recordings have been submitted.

Cutting loose the big boys means that the author, musician, actor, director, or screenwriter is now on his or her own. He or she has to not only create content, but must also convert the content to forms that the buying public will consume. He or she must also promote the creation and in some cases, sell it directly to customers. There are companies, however, that will do the printing, copying, packaging, and handling sales for the creator. In many cases, these companies will be reasonably priced and allow on demand publishing and production. This book will tell the reader what to look out for and how to handle material submission.

Now that the possibilities of success has been discussed, the struggle must also be discussed. Most people don't know this, but the average author sells only about 12 books. These books are usually sold to friends, family, and acquaintances. In many cases, these people never even read the book. They buy the book for the novelty of being able to say that they know a "published author."

For music CD's, less than two and a half percent of albums released in 2009 sold 5000 copies or more. In other words, those who expect to get filthy rich producing and publishing their creations are very likely to be deeply disappointed. However, this does not mean that there will not be any who do get filthy rich. The same forces that bring competition to the big outfits are the same forces that bring the same competition to the small guy. The big guys have huge advertising budgets that can help them stand a little bit above the competition, so they have the advantage in this regard.

If there is such a small chance in making it big, then why get into publishing and production in the first place? This is a good question. A published author can add one more thing to his or her resume in order to stand above other job seekers. A published author may in some cases use his or her book as a credential in lieu of a college degree. In some cases, the publish author may seek college credit based upon the published work.

Audio and video producers also have reasons for production. A church may want to record services so that a wider group of people can be reached. A company may want to do a video feature of a product. A citizen may want to influence government policy. A citizen journalist may want to shed light on corrupt practices. A dissatisfied customer may want to make a complaint known to the public, or a couple may just want their wedding day preserved for posterity. Just as the printing press was very useful in spreading the Good News of the Kingdom, a video or audio production can accomplish the same thing. A book, manual, video, or audio recording may also be produced in order to teach people how to perform a certain task or use a certain product. When this information is distributed on paper media, disc media, or via the Internet, it can save a company money in technical support costs. A well done how to video can be even used to advertise a product or service. There are many reasons why to get into publishing and production. These are just a few.

Chapter 1
Introduction to Production and Publishing

Since very early times, people have always had thoughts and ideas that they wanted to communicate to others. Simply put, media publishing and production is about communication. From the days when Noah and his family stepped off that big boat until today, people have devised ways of communicating to as wide an audience as possible. The good news is that today, we have the tools to reach billions and reach them inexpensively. The bad news is that fact that so do many, many others. Even though we have these tools, we have to compete with others who use the same tools for the attention of our audience. Every person has his or her own favorite way of communicating and receiving information. Some people like to read, others like to watch, and others like to listen. Some like to do two of these or even all three.

Most people's favorite method of receiving information changes throughout the day. For example, someone who is driving through heavy traffic on the way to work would be wise to listen to an audio production instead of reading a book or newspaper. Someone who is a night watchman in a guard shack in the middle of nowhere would be more likely to read. A person relaxing on the beach, at the lake, or waiting for a doctor's appointment will also be more likely to read. A person sitting at home on the computer will be as likely to want to watch or listen as he or she is to read. A person relaxing in the living room or den will most likely to want to watch.

Understanding where, when, how, and why people absorb information is a huge battle. Once the where, when, how, and why is learned, the producer or publisher can then work to provide the method of imparting the information and entertainment desired. The more mediums a producer or publisher is able to use, the greater his or her potential audience. After a few paragraphs of history, each medium of communication will be discussed in the rest of this chapter.

Listening

Listening is one of the oldest ways of receiving information. This method dates back to the very beginning. However, until the past two hundred years, the range of obtaining information through this method was limited to the sound range of the person singing, playing instruments, or speaking. Anything past this hearing range had to be relayed by another person. During the nineteenth century and early twentieth century, this changed. The phonograph, telephone, and the radio were invented. A person could make a recording and send it to someone else thousands of miles away. A person could also make a bunch of phonographs and send them to multiple people. With a radio transmission, one person could reach many people provided they each were in hearing range of the radio receiver. The problem with using these mediums to reach other is the fact that the equipment needed to send out information was very expensive and usually out of the reach of the ordinary people. The person or business that owned the equipment were the ones who decided who could communicate.

As technology advanced, individuals could produce their own cassette tapes and mail them to friends and family around the world. Postage was still expensive, but educating, informing, and entertaining using this method was relative cheap compared to earlier methods. However, cassette tapes still required expensive equipment in order to be mass produced. Even then, quality deteriorated as more copies were made and time wore on.

The next step in the evolution of listening as a method of receiving communication was the audio CD. Once a CD burner was installed in computers, there was real competition to the traditional music media companies. The CD allowed perfect copies of whatever audio needed to be distributed. Now, the main cost for such distribution was postage, packaging, the cost of the blank CD, and wear and tear on the computer and CD burner. This cost still limited many people from becoming independent producers.

The final change that allowed ordinary

individuals to reach a large listening audience was the Internet. The Internet allowed audio files to be transmitted from producer to consumer in mere minutes. The consumer can then copy the audio to his or her favorite device and the use it.

Reading

Reading is another old way of receiving information. Until the last few centuries, however, relatively few people had the privilege of learning how to read. Most people were too hard at work producing the necessities in life rather than having time to learn to read. In addition, until the Gutenberg press was invented, each book or other text had to be individually written page by page and letter by letter. The texts would then have to be physically carried from place to place in order to be seen by many. Once the Gutenberg press was invented, books and other texts could be mass produced. However, the expense and effort required to get the text from one place to the next was still present, and so was the fact that such a relatively few people were able to read. However, the effort required to send text over long distances was greatly reduced in the nineteenth century with the invention of the telegraph. The telegraph, however, required long wires, and putting up these wires was very expensive. Again the rich owned and controlled the method of communication. It was not until the early twentieth century that it became possible for a person of relatively modest means to be able to publish text to a wide audience. The mimeograph machine made that possible, but then again, there was the expense of getting the text from the producer to the consumer. This cost became even cheaper with the advent of the photocopier. Years later, came the fax, the computer printer, the computer bulletin board services, and eventually, the Internet. The Internet made it possible for authors to reach their readers at little to no cost to either.

Watching

Transmitting information or entertainment to those watching is the method that required the most time, effort and skill. From times ancient, the person producing the information or giving the performance would have to be within eyesight and earshot of the audience.

This was true until the late nineteen and early twentieth century. In the nineteen century, the film projector was created. This allowed a producer to reach people thousands of miles away. However, the film reels had to be physically delivered that distance. In addition, the equipment needed to produce film reels was expensive. This put motion picture production out of the reach of the average person. Even when the television was produced and the effort to move visual information was greatly reduced, the equipment still cost too much to be affordable by the common man. It was not until the late twentieth century that video recording became affordable to the common person.

The common person now had the means to produce video and send it to people all over the place. The main expense for doing so was usually postage, the cost of blank tapes, and the wear and tear on the equipment. As years passed, the equipment got cheaper, and the Internet got fast enough to allow video transmission. Again, the Internet and inexpensive equipment make it possible for the common man to reach millions.

Today, we have the Internet and inexpensive

equipment to watch, read, listen, print, and record media.

Does this mean that anything one produces will be gobbled up eagerly by millions? No it doesn't. First, the consumer has to know that the particular content exists. Second, the consumer has to be interested in the content. Third, the content has to be delivered in a form that is accessible by the consumer.

Satisfying each of these conditions is necessary for a person to willingly consume entertainment or information.

When an author publishes a text for his or her readers, he or she should put the text in a form that the reader can and will want to use. A person who lives in a cramped apartment, a military barracks, or is in a hospital will not very likely be able to have a huge collection of books. However, those in a cramped apartment, the military, or hospital may have a laptop computer or a device especially designed to read texts electronically. Having a book published in an electronic format that is compatible with laptop computers and electronic readers should be a priority for the independent author. However, the traditional paperback book is not yet obsolete. There are still many people even in the United States in this day and age who do not have reliable access to the Internet. There are also those who do not like to use a computer nor have the know how to do so. People in prison, for example, may have very little or no access to the Internet or other electronic means. Other people may have a very busy schedule, and the only time they are inclined to absorb information or entertainment is on their way to or from work. In the case where they are driving, it is a bad idea for them to take their eyes off the road to read anything regardless of format. However, if a book is put into an audio form, it would be much more convenient for the customer in this case. It would also be more convenient for a person who is blind or visually impaired. In another case, a person may either not have the money to buy any form of the book, or he or she may not be willing to spend the money. In this case, the book may be posted to the web for consumption. The author may decide to use some form of advertising embedded in the web version in order to attempt to make some money. Works of text and pictures should be in as many forms as possible for customers of all tastes and abilities.

When a musician or other audio producer produces a work, he or she should be mindful of the listener. If the only medium on which the audio recording is produced is a CD, then those who do not have a CD player will be left out. If an audio file is only available for computer download or for digital players, then those without computers or digital players will be left out. Also left out are those who do not, can not, or will not use a computer. Other customers left out are the millions of Americans without broadband Internet. A downloadable audio file that is only available in a form that requires a certain program or operating system in order to work leaves out those who have and use other programs or operating systems. A non musical work should also be put in text format if the producer would like to reach the deaf, hard of hearing, or others who prefer to read instead of listen. Works of audio should be in as many forms as possible for customers of all tastes and abilities.

When a person produces a video, he or she

should be mindful of the audience. If the only medium a video is produced in is DVD, then those who either don't have a DVD player or who don't have it readily available will be left out. If the producer only posts the video on the Internet, then those without broadband Internet access will be left out. A video made available only on an Internet television appliance such as the Roku will leave out everyone who does not have the appliance. A blind person will be unable to watch a video production. However, if there is an audio edition produced, the blind person will not be excluded, and neither will the person commuting to work. If there is text captioning, then the deaf will not miss out on the audio portion of the production. A deaf person will also benefit from a text version. Works of video should be in as many forms as possible for customers of all tastes and abilities.

With all of this said, the producer should look at the costs of making his or her work available in the various formats. The price of each format should reflect the cost of producing that format. For example when the author published, "Tech Tactics Money

Saving Secrets" via Create Space, the selling price was $19.95. For each book that is sold in a bookstore, that amounted to a $2.19 royalty. The Kindle edition of the same book sells for $2.99. For each Kindle edition, the author makes 2.09. The author makes around the same profit either way. If the book is sold via Amazon or Create Space, the author makes more money. There is a desire by the author for a certain minimum return on the investment in labor for each book sold regardless of format.

Some producers and publishers are afraid of making their works available on the Internet in various formats due to piracy. This is definitely a valid concern. It is very easy to copy and redistribute text files, audio files, or video files. It is only slightly more difficult to copy and redistribute digitally restricted formats or even paperback books, CD's, or DVD's. This is due to the fact that anything that can be seen or heard can be copied.

There are programs available that can rip the video and audio from a DVD that has copy protection. There are also very inexpensive flatbed scanners and optical character recognition programs that can be used to convert paperback books into electronic formats for distribution on file sharing networks. There are programs available that will copy a digitally restricted Kindle e-book and allow it to be converted to a PDF file that can be read on just about any computer. It is of the opinion of the author that digital restriction management a.k.a. Digital Rights Management (DRM) will not deter a determined or knowledgeable copyright infringer. However, it may very well frustrate a paying customer who wishes to put a purchased product on another device.

Anything that makes it hard for a customer to use what he or she pays for is not good for the customer or the seller.

This chapter can be summarized in just a few sentences. The art and science of disseminating information and entertainment has improved exponentially over the last century. When content is in as many formats as possible, it can reach many more people who want and desire it. Content should be easily available to paying customers on whatever device they choose to use.

When content is made available to cater to as many people as possible, both the producer and the customer win.

Chapter 2
Outsourcing Production, Publishing, and Sales

One of the best ways of publishing and producing content to tangible media is to get someone else to do it. The reason for this is the fact that bulk printing and copying equipment is very expensive. A DVD duplicating machine that is capable of copying seven DVD's at a time can cost around $1,100. A DVD printer that prints directly to the surface of the copied DVD can cost around $1,200. A combination unit that will both copy and print will run around $2,400. Another consideration is the cost of packaging and shipping the product. If one is handling the orders as well, the time, trouble, and costs of taking the orders, processing credit card, etc. can be much more trouble than it is worth.

There are business that handle the copying, printing, and sales. Some of these businesses do so without huge up front fees. The author or producer still has to take care of any formatting, cover artwork, editing, etc. for many of these businesses. Some of these businesses will also handle these tasks as well. However, they will likely charge a huge fee up front. For the versatile author, musician, or video producer, being able to design eye catching cover art or having someone who can do so inexpensively is a must. Being able to format text, picture, and or video to the specifications of the production or printing company is essential. The good news is the fact that there is plenty of free software out there that does a good job of doing this very thing.

Publish on Demand

Some very good outfits that will actually produce the CD's, DVD's, books, and other media are the publish on demand outfits. These companies work by receiving orders for materials and producing them as needed. If one copy is ordered, one copy is produced and shipped. If the same company receives an order for 1000 copies, the company will produce 1000 copies and ship them to the person or company ordering them. In addition, many publish on demand companies will also take orders directly from customers, handle the billing, and ship the item to the customer. The author or producer has to handle the creative and marketing aspects. Many of these companies will even provide an ISBN or UPC number free of charge to the producer or publisher of the material. The publish on demand company will usually allow the producer or publisher to bring his or her own ISBN or UPC if this is so desired. This is important since most stores will not sell an item without a UPC or ISBN. Publish on demand companies differ from both the traditional and vanity publishing companies due to the fact that their revenue can come from both the author and people besides the author. Publishing or production on demand has an interest in both the creator buying product and services as well as their customers buying product or services. This gives an incentive to these companies to offer sales and promotion channels to their content creators.

Even though there are many advantages to using publish on demand, there are also a few disadvantages. One disadvantage is that the publisher or producer must adhere to the specifications and file formats that are required by the publish on demand company. In many cases, submitted products must also fall withing certain physical sizes. Another disadvantage is the fact that submitted material must conform to content guidelines set by the publish on demand company. This means that in many cases, content instructing people on how to conduct activities not approved by governments (i.e. illegal) will be rejected. It also means that content depicting hard core pornography is also likely to be rejected.

Publish on demand companies are in business to make money. They are not in the business of having to deal with angry police, judges, or other public officials. In many cases, it is possible to get instructions on illegal activity approved by simply making the set of instructions into a story instead of listing step by step instructions on how to disable an alarm system, for example. The material can show a character doing this task step by step. This, however will usually not work with pornography. Some self publishing companies also have aggressive pricing policies in order to shut out the competition.

This means that when a product is sold through and via the company, the company may reserve the right to reduce the price of the product as well as the royalty paid if it finds the same product being sold at a cheaper price at a competing company.

There are many publish on demand companies out there who are willing to handle the actual manufacturing and sales of materials. A few of these as well as their advantages and disadvantages are listed in this chapter. There are surely many others out there, but it would take more than an entire book to cover all of them. The five ones that are the easiest, most inexpensive, and accessible are covered in this chapter.

Amazon

Amazon started out as an on-line bookstore. However, Amazon has expanded its business to include much more than books. Amazon has also gotten into the book, CD, and DVD manufacturing business as well through spin off companies. Amazon produces the Kindle e-book reading device. In order to market this device effectively, Amazon has also had to supply a huge inventory of electronic books. Books can be submitted to Amazon in electronic format, and such form will be converted into the format used by Kindle. The publisher of the electronic book will receive from thirty to seventy percent royalties for each electronic book copy sold. Amazon also allow authors to publish free books. However authors should be aware that Amazon forbids the use of the advertising supported model, This means that an author cannot just place banner advertisements through the electronic book. Even so, Amazon provides a marketplace in which to sell electronic books. To sell more electronic books, Amazon even offers software that allows computers, tablet devices, and phones to function as Kindle readers. This gives Amazon the opportunity to distribute even more electronic media. Amazon's e-book sales program is called Kindle Direct Publishing, and it is available at http://kdp.amazon.com. Setting up an e-book seller's account through Amazon is free. Amazon also allows the self publishing of books, DVD's, and CD's. However, these are produced via subsidiary companies that will be discussed in this chapter.

Barnes and Noble

Barnes and Noble is another book store that competes with Amazon. Barnes and Noble also has its own e-book reader. The Barnes and Noble e-book reader is called the Nook. Barnes and Noble also pays royalties on electronic books that it sells for the Nook. An author or publisher can also release free books for the Nook as well. Setting up an account with Barnes and Noble is free. All the user has to do is visit http://www.bn.com/pubit and sign up for the service.

Cafe Press

Cafe Press is a company that allows people to create images and text that can be printed on items such as clothing, cups, pins, jewelry, and other items. Such items are then manufactured on demand just like the books, CD's, and DVD's are manufactured by the publish on demand companies. Cafe Press allows such items to be produced with very little if any set up costs. Cafe Press has a website that can be reached at http://www.cafepress.com. Cafe Press is a good company to use for generating promotional items.

Create Space

Create Space is a part of Amazon. Create Space provides services for both publishing and production of paperback books, CD's, and DVD's. Not only does Create Space publish these media, but it can also sell this media through its parent company, Amazon. Another service that Create Space offers is the option of providing a Universal Product Code UPC or International Standard Book Number ISBN at no cost to those who submit products for publication or production. Create Space also offers a website for sales as well as the options of expanded distribution via other sales outlets. Create Space offers flexible sizing options for books, and several packaging options for CD's and DVD's. The author highly recommends this company due to the fact that he has published material through this company and has been extremely satisfied. Create Space's website is http://www.createspace.com.

Lightning Press

Lightning Press is yet another print on demand outfit. One thing that Lightning Press will do that many others will not is print hardbound books. Unlike some of the other print on demand outfits, Lightning Press does not have pricing information available on its site. However, for those who wish to have hardbound books printed may take a look at this company and requesting a quote. This can be done by visiting http://lightning-press.com.

Lulu

Lulu, like Create Space, is another printing house that many self published authors use. Lulu has the advantage of not being an Amazon company. Amazon's practices of offering customers very good deals irks many competitors. Many of them refuse to carry Amazon's books in their stores. Those who wish to sell their books in most brick and mortar stores rather than on-line may want to have a look at using Lulu as well. Lulu can be accessed at http://www.lulu.com.

Smashwords

Smashwords is another worthwhile electronic book publishing outfit, This company also provides a free ISBN. One should check out this company by visiting http://www.smashwords.com.

Disc Makers

Disc Makers is a CD and DVD production company. This company will copy CD and DVD media as well chosen packaging and send it to the person requesting the service. This company only manufactures the product. It does not provide sales channels, or UPC information. However for small or limited distribution, this company is definitely an option. This company can also be used in conjunction with other production on demand services. If the media is identical, one may even decide to use the UPC that is supplied by Disc Makers. Disc Makers website can be reached at http://www.discmakers.com.

Vanity Presses

A vanity press or vanity publisher is a term used to describe a publishing company where the author or content producer has to pay to have their work published. The vanity press differs from a traditional publisher in the sense that a traditional publisher derives its revenue from the sales of books to customers other than the creator. The vanity press derives its revenue from the creator of the content. The vanity press likely derived its name from appealing to the fact that people like to see themselves published and their name shown on a physical product. Since the vanity press is usually not selective about what it publishes, the same prestige is not attributed to authors and producers who use the services of a vanity press as those who are published through a traditional publishing company. In addition, the vanity press usually charges much more to publish and author's work compared to publish on demand companies. Since Vanity production and publishing companies make their revenue from the creators of content, they are usually not concerned if such content sells or sits in the basement of the writer, musician, or actor. Because of the high investment costs for content creators, the use of vanity presses or production companies is not recommended by the author. In order to find out which companies are vanity presses can be done by entering "list of vanity presses" into the search window of many major search engines such as Google, Ask, or Yahoo. Companies such as Create Space, Lulu, and other book printing companies may show up on this list as well, but these companies should be considered book printing outfits rather than vanity presses. Like it is previously stated, this author publishes his work through Create Space and has found this company to be a good deal.

Why Not Traditional Publishers or Producers?

The traditional publishing or production company is usually very selective in what it publishes or produces due to the fact that it has spent much time, effort, and money cultivating its reputation as a source of high quality work. This also means that writers, musicians, or actors who want to sell their work through a traditional publisher or production company must show the company that his or her work will be of the highest quality. This means that the writer, musician, or actor must display his or her credentials, previous works, and any other thing that will help him or her establish credibility. A traditional publisher or producer not only must be sure of the quality of the work of the writer, musician, or actor, it must also have a good reason to believe that such work will sell enough copies to be profitable to the company. When a traditional publishing, movie, or music production outfit takes on a new writer, musician, or actor, it is making a huge gamble. This is due to the fact that the the traditional outfit must not only produce the media to be sold, but it must also promote the new writer, musician, or actor. If the work flops, then the publishing or production outfit is not only out of the money it has invested, but the company's reputation also takes a hit. Traditional publishing and production companies have to hire employees to separate bad quality work from good quality work. These employees require wages to be paid, and those wages come out of a budget. Budgets require that only a finite number of employees be hired to screen new incoming work. This means that the employees screening work do not have the time to examine each work thoroughly. In many cases, submitted work may only receive only a few moments worth of examination. In other cases, work may not be even examined. Publishing and production outfits are not too concerned with the frustrations of prospective writers, actors, or musicians. They are concerned mainly with making money. This is true with any for profit business.

Other People with the Equipment

Sometimes a writer, musician, or actor, may have a friend, acquaintance, or family member who has his or her own copying or mass printing and binding equipment that can be utilized. If this is the case, then it may be a good idea to use this source of production to test the waters and see if a work has potential. Such production may also be used in conjunction with services offered by publishing or production on demand companies. Advantages of using such local resources is the fact that product may be quickly produced in a pinch. For products such as CD's and DVD's the cost may be much less than what the produce on demand services cost.

This chapter explained the different types of production and publishing companies as well as the advantages and disadvantages of using each. Using outsourced publishing, production, registration, and sales services help the writer, musician, or actor concentrate on what he or she does best, and that is create. Using outsourced services also reduces the initial investment for equipment and supplies. The next chapters explain how to create information and entertainment and convert it into a format usable by both home production and publishing equipment as well as outsourced services.

In House Production and Publishing

In most cases it is highly recommended that the actual production and publication of CD's, DVD's, books, posters, and other printed material be outsourced as explained in the previous section. However, there are cases where it may be better to produce a product in house. Such cases where it may be better to produce in house is when only a few copies are needed, the content is needed quickly, or the content is extremely confidential or frowned upon by the jurisdiction where it is produced. In such cases, it may be better to produce what is needed in house.

The equipment used in publishing in house CD's and DVD's can be either expensive custom equipment such as CD/DVD printing and duplicating machines, or it can be as inexpensive as one or more computers with CD or DVD writable drives. An ink jet or laser printer can be used to print information labels that can be attached to duplicated CD's or DVD's The quality of the playable media can be nearly as good as that of production companies. Printed material, however, is another story. While it is possible to use an ink-jet, laser, or even dot matrix printer to churn out pages, the pages be somehow bound together. In addition, most commercial books have a high quality cover and spine. Posters that are printed from ordinary home or small office printers generally have to be assembled from individual sheets of paper. A close look at a poster created in this manner will show where the individual sheets of paper are attached to one another. However, for a quick guerrilla advertising campaign, this method may work very well.

Chapter 3
Producing Audio and Music

This chapter provides information on how to record, produce, edit, convert, and distribute audio media and files of many different types. This chapter describes not only different recording environments, but it also discusses different types of audio recording equipment, free software that can be used to extract, edit and convert audio to needed formats, as well as options for distribution.

The Environment

Sound recordings can be recorded, stored, and produced in many different ways. Despite what many people think, it is possible to get high quality audio with little background noise without putting together or renting an expensive studio. In many cases all that is needed is a decent quality camcorder or digital audio recording equipment and a quiet, outdoor environment. On a day with little or no wind, the audio recorded outdoors can sound very good. The author knows of at least one musician who sometimes records his music this way. In other cases an impromptu studio can be set up in a spare bedroom, shed, cave, basement, warehouse, or other building. Wherever recording is done, there should be facilities that provide electric power if it is needed for instruments, amplifiers, recording equipment or computers. In many cases, all that is needed is the battery power that is attached to the digital recording device.

Indoor Recording Studios

When setting up an indoor studio for recording, one should be aware of ambient noise. A good way to gage ambient noise is to record about five to ten minutes without singing, talking, or playing any instruments. The participants need to be as silent as possible while performing other tasks related to recording. After this recording is completed, one should listen to the recording and try to identify any background noise.

Back ground noise can come from many sources such as the hum from power supplies, noise from temperature control products, fans, plumbing, other house noises, noises from traffic, or noises from people in other rooms, etc. Once noises are identified, one can take measure to turn off equipment that generates it or move such equipment away from microphones. Carpet, foam rubber, and other soft material can also be used to block or absorb sound.

What this text does not cover is musical instruments, equipment, speakers, or amplifiers. Those are considered by the author to be related to performance and not production. However, when connecting the output of any of these devices to the audio recording device, one should check to make sure that he or she uses the correct output. Connecting, for example, the amplifier output meant for a 100 watt speaker into the the microphone input on a camcorder will very likely damage the camcorder as well as the amplifier. In such a case where the appropriate output is not available or the correct attenuation device cannot be found, it is best to record from the cam-corder's built in microphone.

Acquiring Audio

There are many ways sound can be acquired. Sometimes, it is recorded to an analog tape deck, and the output of such a device is fed into a computer. Other times, it is recorded to a digital camcorder, and the video file is uploaded to a computer. In that case, a program is used to strip the audio from the video and save the audio. Quality recordings can be even made with such a device as the iPod Nano Video. Sometimes, even smartphones are used to make a recording. There are so many different devices from which audio can be obtained that it is no possible to cover them all in this text. However what will be covered are the basic methods of getting the audio from the device into the computer where it can be extracted, edited, and converted to the formats needed.

Yet, in other cases, the audio may be acquired by downloading it from the Internet. Videos can be downloaded from You Tube or other video sites and the audio can be then extracted. There are plenty of programs or web browser extensions that can allow this to be done. When audio or video is downloaded from the Internet to be re-distributed, one should make sure that he or she has the rights to use the content in this manner.
There are several ways audio can be inputted

into the computer for use. One of these ways is for it to be played into the microphone or line input on the sound card. Another way it can get into the computer is for it to be downloaded from a camcorder via USB or Fire wire cable. Yet another way is for a memory card to be removed from the camcorder, inserted into a card reader slot on a computer, and the video file directly accessed. In the the last two cases, it will not only be necessary to access the video file, but it will also be necessary to extract the audio from the video. There is free software that can handle this task.

Alis (audio recording)

The Alis Audio Recording tool is a program that allows a user to simultaneously capture and record audio using one or more sound cards as audio sources. This tool is written in Java and requires that the Java Virtual machine be first installed on the computer. Most computers have Java installed, but if a computer does not, then Java can be downloaded from http://java.com. Like a few other programs listed in this book, Alis does not come with an installer. Instead, it is distributed as a zip file which must be extracted with a program such as 7-zip.

Audacity (audio editing)

Audacity is a great sound editing program with many different features that allow the insertion of sound clips, the deletion of undesirable sound clips, as well as being able to insert periods of silence into an audio track. Audacity is an open source, multi-platform editing program that is available for Windows, Mac-OS, and Linux. It is a free download and is available at http://audacity.sourceforge.net/.

Audacity can open and export to files with aiff, wav, gsm, mp3, ogg, and flac formats (or extensions). This gives the user the ability to create and edit files that are compatible with CD and DVD's, telephone systems, computers, and mp3 players. Depending upon the type of sound card in a computer, it can also be used to record streaming audio. Audacity is a relatively simple to use program. It is also simple to install. When downloading Audacity, one should make sure that they are downloading the correct program for their operating system. There is a difference between Windows XP, Windows Vista, and Windows 7 as well as the different versions of MAC OSX.

Another relatively handy feature Audacity has is the ability to provide author, performer, song title, and other information to be embedded in the audio file itself. This information is not actually heard when an audio file is being played, but this information may be shown on a player's display. When editing a track, a user can click on File and then select meta data editor to edit the embedded file information.

Another good part of Audacity is the fact that it is well documented with many tutorials available on-line. One good place to start is by visiting the tutorial offered by the creators of Audacity themselves. This tutorial can be found by visiting http://audacity.sourceforge.net/manual-1.2/index.html. Other tutorials can be found by searching the Internet for "Audacity Tutorials." Searching You Tube will provide a huge number of video examples on how to use this great piece of software.

Avidemux (audio extraction)

Avidemux is an excellent program that is used by the author in producing sermon videos for his congregation. Avidemux ix also multi platform and is capable of running on Linux, Windows, Mac-OS, and BSD. Avi demux can open many different video files and allow the audio to be extracted and saved to the aac, pcm (wav), ac3, mp2, mp3, and Vorbis formats.

Installation is a bit different than with most programs at least as far as its Windows version is concerned. Avidemux is distributed as a zip file. The file is downloaded to the user's computer and a program such as 7-Zip is used to extract the contents to a directory. The user must then manually navigate to the newly created directory and then click on the Avidemux application in order to run the program.

To extract an audio track from a video and save it to the computer is relatively simple. The program is executed per the instructions in the above paragraph. Once the program is opened, the user will click on File, Open, and then select the video file from which he or she wants the audio. After the file is selected and opened, the user may be asked a question about frame accuracy. It is good to choose, "Yes," if the purpose is only to extract the audio. If the user is asked if he or she wants to index the file, he or she should also choose to do so. If there are a series of files with consecutive filenames in the same directory as the file to be used, the user may be asked if he or she wants to append the files. He or she should choose no unless he or she want the audio from all of these in a long track. After the file is opened, extracting the audio is simple. Under the audio heading on the left side of the program, the user clicks on the drop down menu and selects the proper format.

If the user want to use the wav format, he or she should select PCM. At the top of the window, the user then clicks on audio and chooses Save. The user then navigates to the folder where the file is to be saved and then types in a filename a period, and then wave. An example of this is myfile.wav. The user then should click the "Save" button. It will take a few second to minutes to extract the audio. The audio is now in a format where it can be edited with the audio editing program.

Like Audacity, Avidemux has plenty of both audio and video tutorials on its use. A simple search using the words, "Avidemux tutorial" on most search engines will provide many of these tutorials. Avidemux is a good program for acquiring audio that is recorded by video devices such as camcorders, video iPods, and other such devices. It is also good for extracting audio from downloaded videos.

Handbrake (audio extraction and video transcoding)

Handbrake is yet another free, multi-platform, open source program that is available for Windows, Linux, and the Mac-OS.
Handbrake allows a person to extract video files from non-encrypted DVD's, allows subtitles to be added to video files, converts videos from one format to another, and even allows audio to be extracted and saved from a video file.. Hand Brake can be downloaded by visiting http://handbrake.fr/. There are plenty of text and video tutorials on how to

use Handbrake to accomplish these many tasks. These can be found by searching for Handbrake tutorials on any search engine. Individual tasks such as how to add subtitles to video can also be found by searching the Internet using terms such as, "Handbrake subtitles tutorial."

Sox

Sox is another program that can be used for creating various audio formats. It is also free, open source, and supports Linux, Windows, and Mac-OS. Unlike the other conversion applications discussed in this chapter, Sox is a command line program and requires that the user to know how to use and type in parameters in order to convert file formats.

Sox is great for people who write their own batch files or scripts that convert software automatically. It is not recommended for novice users. Sox can be downloaded by visiting http://sox.sourceforge.net/. There are also plenty of web tutorials on how to use this software that can be found by searching for "Sox Sound Exchange tutorial." The search terms stated in the last sentence are recommended in order to filter out irrelevant results.

Download helper

Download Helper is not a self contained program but rather a Firefox browser extension that allows users to download videos from many different sites such as Youtube, Vivemo, Veoh, etc. It literally allows video to be downloaded from hundreds of different sites. Download Helper can be installed by visiting http://www.downloadhelper.net and following the instructions. The Firefox web browser is required in order to use download Helper, and that can be downloaded by visiting http://www.getfirefox.com.

Downloading videos is as simple as clicking on the Download helper button and selecting which video to download. In some cases where advertisements are played before the desired video, it may be necessary to wait for the desired video to start playing before clicking on the Download Helper button.

CD/DVD media

Even though there are so many audio files available on-line, there is still the need for audio CD's due to the fact that many vehicles have sound systems that only play regular CD's. In addition, many people who do not know how to use other digital formats still rely on the CD. Players with the ability to display information such as the Title, Album, and artists will make a person's home produced CD look very impressive if this information is encoded into the audio files on the CD. This information coding can be done With the Audacity program.

In order to produce CD's, a CD burning program is required to put the audio files onto the CD in a way that they can be played by CD players. Several free programs are available that can do this. Another thing to consider is using a printer that prints directly onto CD's. Another way to create a CD cover is to use stick on labels These labels can be purchased at most any office supply shop. When stick on labels are used, one can use a digital scanner to obtain a template that can be used to create the cover design.

The label sheets are fed into a scanner (without peeling the backing paper of course), and a graphics file showing the label side is retrieved. The graphics file can be used as a template to know where the boundaries are for the label itself. Such a template will allow a computer user to use an ordinary graphics editing program to crate a cover that will be within the boundaries of the of the portion of the label that actually goes on the CD itself.

In addition to using self created CD cover template, a user can use any number of CD cover design templates or websites to help with the job.

In order to write CD's using a computer, the computer must be equipped with a CD drive that is capable of burning CD's. In addition, there must also be a program installed on the computer that will handle this task. Many computers which come with CD burners will have a program such as Roxio, Nero, Cyber Link or similar commercial software to handle the task. If a CD/DVD burner is installed into the computer after purchase, it will most likely come with CD/DVD burning software. However, sometimes an operating system will have been re-installed, and the CD/DVD burning software may not be found and the original disc misplaced. If this is the case, there are many free programs that will allow users to burn CD's. Some of these are listed here in this chapter. CD/DVD burning programs are usually non cross platform. That means that Programs written for Microsoft Windows will not usually work on Linux and Mac-OS and vice versa. Therefore, it is best to find software that will work for the user's operating system. There are plenty of choices of free software that does a good job.

Infrarecorder

One CD/DVD burning program that is for Windows only is called InfraRecorder. It is available for download by visiting http://infrarecorder.org/. Infrarecorder will burn both CD's and DVD's and more importantly will allow a user to burn both iso and cue images to the CD or DVD. It can also produce copies of other CD's and unencrypted DVD's.

To burn an audio CD one has to open the program, Click on File, choose "New Project" and then Audio CD. After that, he or she drags the wav file of the audio to be burned into the project and burn. There are different types of wave file, and if Infrarecorder complains about a file, then Audacity can be used to convert the file so that it can be used by Infrarecorder. Again, there are plenty of tutorials on how to use Infrarecorder. These can be found by simply searching the Internet for Infrarecorder tutorials.

CDBurner XP

Another program that can be used on Windows to burn CD's is called, "CDBurner XP." This program is also free, but it is not open source. The reason that it is not open source according to the creator is the fact that it uses third party software licenses. The program can be downloaded by visiting http://cdburnerxp.se/. CDBurner XP will allow the user to create data CD/DVD's, create audio CD/DVD's, copy CD/DVD's, and more. Unfortunately, this program is Windows only.

K3B

K3B is a Linux based CD burning program. It can be downloaded by visiting http://www.k3b.org/ or by the Linux distribution package manager. K3b has the ability to create audio CD's, video CD's, data CD's, mixed-mode CD's, and eMovix CD's. K3B Will also burn DVD data projects, eMovix DVD's, and will burn (but not author) regular video DVD's. K3B will copy these mediums as well. K3B will format CD and DVD rewritable mediums as well. It will even rip most video and audio CD's and DVD's. K3B is highly recommended by the author to people who use Linux

One thing to keep in mind when burning CD's or DVD's is the fact that many CD/DVD burners in computers will have higher burn speeds than can be handle by many CD or DVD players. Because of this fact, it is best to burn CD's and DVD's at the slowest speed possible in order to ensure compatibility with more devices. There are also several kinds of CD's both read only and writable on the market. These include the pressed CD's that are read only (music CD's sold in stores) known as CD-DA, audio or music CD-R (recorable one time only), audio or music CD-RW (can be rewritten multiple times), data CD-R (recordable one time only), and data CD-RW (recordable one time only). Data CD-R's and CD-RW's can can be used to record music in the same ways as the ones labeled for audio recording. The main difference between the two is the fact that the ones labeled for audio use are taxed at a higher rate in some countries in order to subsidize their music industries. Another feature available on some CD's is the fact that they may have a directly printable label surface. These are used to manufacture CD's that can be printed by a specialized (and expensive) printer. Another variant are CD's that have a laser printable surface, and these are known as Light Scribe CD's.

Distribution

Audio can and is distributed in many different ways, it can be distributed via CD's, or on-line as computer files such as CD, wma files, mp3 files, or wav files. They can even be distributed as custom ring tones for phones. The many different ways of distributing audio is available to just about any one. The Internet is an all time equalizer for big and small media producers.

CD's can be distributed locally, mailed, or even put on file sharing networks to be downloaded. Mp3's can be published to one of the many music sites out there such a http://www.emusic.com, on an Internet radio station site such as Pandora, or via email or a file sharing network. Ring tones can also be distributed on-line or by sending as part of a text message. Each of these formats can also be copied from computer to computer via devices such as thumb drives, etc.

This chapter gives several tips on how to create and distribute audio files. Due to the fact that programs, technology, and service come, go, and change on a daily basis, it is really impossible to put specific step by step instructions on how do operate each program, sign up for each service, or contract with third party vendors without this book becoming out of date within a week of publication. The good news, however is the fact that such helpful information is available on the Internet in the form of text or video tutorials. This book, however will give the layman a good start to becoming a audio media creator and publisher. Chapter six give much more information on how to sell and distribute media in all forms over the Internet.

Chapter 4
Producing Video

Producing and distributing video has to be one of the most exciting aspects of production and publication. Today, with modern software, it becomes possible for people to produce professional looking videos with even free software. Such videos can be posted to one or more of the many video distribution sites, made into DVD's, or made available through one of the many Internet Streaming Devices such as the Roku, Tivo, Apple, TV, Google TV, via phones, or via some of the many other devices. This describes what is needed to acquire, edit, convert, and distribute video media.

Video production has been getting easier with the assistance of technology, but there are also other factors that contribute to good quality video. One of these is proper lighting. Video recording equipment needs proper lighting in order to produce good looking, professional quality videos. Lighting equipment can be acquired from many different places on the Internet, or it can be obtained in local stores.

Light that is shined on the set should be evenly distributed and should also ensure that the subject as well as the rest of the scene is properly illuminated. One popular, low cost method of shooting a video involves shooting outdoors on a bright day. If blue or green chroma key cloth, regular cloth, paper, or painted surface is used, a good quality scene can be added in later using software. This method is done best when there is no camera movement used. The subjects in the scene should avoid wearing colors that match the color of the chroma key cloth or other background used.

Acquiring Video

There are currently tens of thousand of ways of acquiring video for use in video production. These include cameras, camcorders, web cameras, cell phones, tablet computers, video acquisition interfaces, downloading from the Internet, and ripping it from current media (with permission, of course). When using such devices, it is best to read the included user manual before using the device. If this manual is not available, then it can usually be downloaded by searching for the brand or model number of the device to be used on-line.

Getting Video to the Computer

In many cases, such media can be easily transferred from the device to the computer using the free software that is included with the device or computer. Many cameras and other video recording devices listed in this section can be connected to a computer using a USB cable. Some of these devices need to be put into transfer mode. This is usually done by pressing a button on the device, and in many cases, the device will go into transfer mode automatically when connected to a computer. In some cases, this transfer can occur with the use of what is called an SD card. Whether a USB cable or a SD card is used, once connected or plugged into a computer, the computer will usually recognize the plugged in device as a portable hard drive and will assign a drive letter or mount point to the device. It is then up to the user to locate where the video can be found on the device. One precaution that needs to be mention is the fact that one should never unplug the cable or SD card without first instructing the computer to dismount the device. In Windows, this is usually accomplished by clicking on a little USB icon located in the system tray and then choosing safely remove device from the resulting pop up menu. Most Linux distributions use a very similar method for un-mounting media devices.

This section gives some of the information, advantages and disadvantages of each method of acquiring video.

Cameras

Digital cameras with video recording capabilities is one method that can be used to acquire video for the use in production. The advantages of using a digital camera with video capabilities is the fact that the camera may be already available. In other words, such a camera will do if for example a person does not have the funds to purchase a camcorder.

One main disadvantage is the fact that the

camera my be capable of only taking short clips or may not have features specifically for capturing video such as microphones to catch any sound that goes along with the video.

Other limiting factors may include a reduced frame rate. Another limiting factor may be a limited choices is aspect ratios (Width of video to height of video). Some cameras, however, will take great quality videos.

Camcorders

Using a camcorder is really the best way of acquiring digital video's for producing video's. This is due to the fact that these devices already have the features needed for shooting raw footage such as higher frame rate, audio capture, selectable aspect ratios, and storage to handle the videos captured. The price of camcorders range from less than a hundred dollars all the way to tens of thousands of dollars. One thing that may need to be pointed out is that most digital camcorder today allow the used of memory cards that are called, "SD Cards." For computers, most any kind of SD card is usable. For digital camcorders, this is not the case. This is due to the fact that video cameras can send video information to the SD card faster than the card can save it. In such cases, the resulting video file will either be missing frames, be corrupted, or be missing altogether. It is a very good idea to read the camcorder's user manual before purchasing such memory cards to ensure one of the right quality is obtained. If the user manual has been lost or thrown away, it can still usually be looked up on the Internet or can be found by visiting the camcorder's manufacturer's website.

When considering a camcorder for the use of video production, there are several things that need to be considered. These include software compatibility, storage capability (how, and how much video can be stored), mounting capability (can it be mounted to a tripod), microphone input jacks (so it can be connected to a sound system), video quality, aspect ratio, etc. Another thing that needs to be considered when purchasing a camera is whether accessories such as tripods, carrying cases, green or blue background cloth (for chroma key effect), gimbal stabilizers (cheap if home made), etc will be needed. These accessories can mean the difference between a quality, professional looking video or one that was shot by a rank amateur.

Webcams

Web cameras, or webcams have also been used to make many video's. Web cameras are usually the ones that connect to a computer via an USB cable. These camera were originally intended for video chat and teleconferencing. However, they have become useful for many other things. They vary in video quality, aspect ratio, whether they have audio capabilities, and frame rate. Web cameras capture picture and individual video frames and sends these to the computer via USB cable for processing. The acquisition software determines if the computer captures each of these frames at the web camera's maximum capability or at a reduced rate. This means that the quality of a webcam is determined by both hardware capabilities and software capabilities.

Cell Phones

Cell phones are used to capture some of the most candid footage known to modern history. Cellphone videos can be uploaded or emailed to other phone users, websites, or via cable to a computer. Cell phone cameras also vary in the quality of video produced. However, one of the biggest advantages of a cell phone camera is the fact that the camera is always available when the user carries his or her phone. This means that users are more able to capture videos quickly as a situation arises. Another advantage is that in some cases, videos from cell phone cameras can be instantly uploaded in the event of imminent confiscation of the device. One disadvantage of cell phone video cameras is the fact that most cell phone cameras have poor automatic focusing capabilities. These cameras are often, "just good enough."

Clandestine Devices

Clandestine video devices are designed so that they can record video without the subject of the video being aware of the recording process. Clandestine recording devices can look like a pen, watch, alarm clock, thumb drive, sunglasses, or any other gadget. In fact, an iPod Nano video device has been used by the author to catch clandestine videos

of a man made disaster. These devices can
mean the difference of a citizen journalist
getting the story or getting thrown in jail.

Tablet Computers

Tablet computers, especially the Apple iPad
is all the rage today. Most of the newer
versions of these devices now sport a camera.
These cameras like cellular telephone
cameras have the same advantage of being
available. This also means that a person can
capture a candid video in a near instant. The
quality of a tablet computer varies just like
that of a cellular phone camera. Videos shot
on these cameras can in many cases also be
uploaded to the Internet in case of possible
confiscation.

Video Acquisition Interfaces

Another way to get video is to record it
directly from the airwaves or to load it from
an old analog device. To do this requires
some form of video capture interface such as
a TV tuner or video input card. These card
are usually available as plug in devices for

expansion slots on a computer's motherboard or as an USB device. Such interfaces may be able to utilize the full capability of the analog device, or they may only be able to utilize a part of it. These acquisition devices are just another option available to a would be producer.

Downloading

Another way of acquiring video for use in a project is by downloading it. Videos can be downloaded from video site such as You Tube, Vimeo, Metacafe, among many others. Downloading video material is easy once the proper software is to be had. The good news is the fact that this software can be had for free.

One tool commonly used was mentioned before in the audio chapter of this book, and that tool is a Firefox browser extension called, "Download Helper." Download Helper can be installed by visiting http://www.downloadhelper.net and following the instructions. The Firefox web browser is required in order to use Download Helper, and that can be downloaded by visiting http://www.getfirefox.com. A stand alone program for downloading videos is YouTube downloader which is available by visiting http://freefilesdownloader.net/.

Vuze

A peer to peer file sharing tool that allows the downloading of videos is called Vuze. Vuze can be downloaded by visiting http://www.vuze.org/.

Ripping

Another way of acquiring video is by ripping it. Ripping involves reading the video from a DVD, Video CD, or other medium and writing it to the computer in a form that is usable to other programs. Ripping video's for use in producing other videos is somewhat controversial due to the fact that most video DVD's and Blue Ray Discs are sold for a profit. However, if a user has written permission from the producer of the DVD, then he or she is free to rip to his or her heart's content. A copy protected DVD has twice the file size as the same non-encrypted counterpart. There are several programs that can be used for ripping both encrypted (copy protected) and unencrypted (non copy protected) DVD's. These include DVDx, DVDshrink, and lxDvdRip

DVDx

DVDx can be downloaded by visiting http://www.labdv.com/dvdx/. DVDx is a free, open source program that runs on Windows, Linux, and Mac OSX. It is said that this program can rip both encrypted and non ecrypted DVD's.

DVDShrink

DVDShrink can be downloaded by visiting http://www.dvdshrink.org/. DVDShrink is free, but is not open source. It runs on Windows only. DVDShrink is one of the most popular programs that Windows users use to rip videos from DVD's. This program can rip video from both unencrypted and encrypted DVD's

lxDvdRip

LxDvdRip is a command line tool to make a

copy from a video DVD. Using lxDvdRip, one can backup just the main feature without the menu or the whole DVD. Unfortunately, lxDvdRip is only available for Linux. It can be downloaded by visiting http://sourceforge.net/p/lxdvdrip/wiki/Home/

Shooting Techniques

When a camcorder is used for acquiring a video, the videographer has much more control over the quality of the video. The videographer will need to pay attention to several factors when taking a shot. A shot is a segment of video that is acquired between the time the video starts recording to the time it is stopped. One of the most important of these is framing. The frame is the video that the videographer sees in the viewfinder.
Scene selection or composition shows the lay out of everything in the frame such as the subject, the background, lighting, and the rest of the environment.

When a scene or subject is introduced, it is usually best to start with a wide area shot in order to give the viewer a sense of the subject's surroundings. This wide area shot should be shown while the audience is being introduced to the story. After the story or interview begins, the videographer usually should concentrate on the subject and his or her immediate environment.

Video editing

After video is acquired, it must then be edited. Editing allows undesirable portions to be deleted and effects and transitions to be added. In many cases, over an hour's worth of video can be recorded with only a minute of it appearing in the final product. This is what commonly happens in TV newsrooms all over the country. Good video editing software such a majority of the ones listed in this chapter can be used to produce a show with multiple views and an animated background that looks similar to that of the Nancy Grace Show.

Effects such as Chroma key (also know as blue or green screen) is also included or is available for most of the video editing products listed in this chapter.

Individual software programs are discussed later in this chapter, but first this chapter will describe some of the transitions and effects commonly used in video editing. These effects can be anything from really mundane to something absolutely spectacular. An effect is something that alters the way a video looks such as making it brighter, darker, louder, quieter, color to black and white, etc. A transition is the way a video clip or shot merges, joins, or bleed through to another clip or shot. Any video editing software that is worth a darn will include both effects and transitions. This book provides general instruction on how to get started publishing and producing content. To provide specific, detailed instructions on how to use each software package is beyond the scope of this book. However, for each program listed, there are many tutorials available on-line that will provide the required instructions. For example, one can use a search engine to find tutorials on how to use Cinelerra by simply typing in the words, "Cinelerra tutorial," "How to use Cinelerra," or to use a specific feature such as chroma key, "how to use chroma key in Cinelerra." Some very good as well as free programs for video editing are listed next.

Cinelerra

Cinelerra is available for both Mac OSX and Linux. Cinelerra is a free nonlinear video editing application that allows multi-track video and audio editing. It also has many effects and transitions, and more can be added by downloading additional plug ins. Cinelerra is available by visiting http://heroinewarrior.com/ or by installing from distribution package manager.

iMovie

iMovie is a nonlinear video editing application specifically for Mac OSX. IMovie is designed to be relatively easy to use and comes with many transitions, effects, and video templates. IMovie comes already installed on most modern Apple Macintosh based computers. One can learn more by visiting http://www.apple.com/ilife/imovie/.

Kdenlive

Kdenlive is available for BSD, Mac OSX, and

Linux It is available by visiting
http://www.kdenlive.org.   Kdenlive is a
very feature rich nonlinear video editing
application that is capable of many special
effects. It can do chroma key effects, cartoon
effects, allow multiple video windows in the
final video output and much more. It is
comparable to some of the thousand dollar
professional video editing applications. One
note to make with Kdenlive is the fact that it
is best to split the audio from the video and
edit the audio and video as separate tracks.
This is due to an annoying quirk in Kdenlive
where the video can get out of sync with the
audio (unless a separate audio track is used).

Windows Movie Maker

Windows Movie Maker is somewhat capable
and has several features that come installed
with the program or can be downloaded as
plug ins. Windows Movie Maker XP is
available as part of Windows XP Service
Pack 3 Information about installing Movie
Maker, if it is not already installed can be
found   by   visiting
http://windows.microsoft.com/en-
US/windows-xp/help/moviemaker/make-

movies-with-movie-maker. Movie maker comes with both Vista and Windows 7.

VideoLAN Movie Creator

VideoLAN Movie Creator is another nonlinear video editing application that is in early development. It is a free and open source application that is showing promise. While this book generally list only tried and true applications, the group working on this product has designed many other high quality applications, and the quality of this application should also be superb once everything comes together. This application is designed to work with many platforms including Windows, Linux MacOS, and BSD. One can try out Movie Creator by visiting http://www.videolan.org/vlmc/. However, since this project is still in the early stages of development, one should check the site often to get new releases and bug fixes. This is a very promising project by reputable developers, and the author is very optimistic that this program will be an exceptional application.

Virtualdub

VirtualDub is a video capture/processing utility for both 32-bit and 64-bit Windows platforms As of the time of this writing, it is not available for Linux or Mac OSX.
Virtualdub can be downloaded by visiting http://www.virtualdub.org/.

Wax

Wax is a high performance and flexible video compositing and special effects program and includes plug-ins for Sony Vegas, Pure Motion EditStudio and Adobe Premiere. Wax allows the creation of special effects such as 3-d text, shatter, particle generation, and Rotomate. It also allows the embedding of certain 3-d models from files including . 3ds, md2, and ms3d. Wax is available for Windows only. It can be downloaded by visiting http://www.debugmode.com/wax/.

ZS4

ZS4 Video Editor is a video editing and compositing program designed to combine a variety of media types into one or more output formats. Get ZS4 at http://www.zs4.net/.

Video Conversion

Video files come in many different formats and file names. These formats include avi, mpg, mp4, mov, wmv, etc. Even these file names are only what are called, "containers." A container is an encoded video in addition to all of the information about the video that is required in order to play the video. One can think of the container format in a similar manner as a zip file. When a group of related files are packaged as a single zip file, the concept is similar to the video, audio, subtitles, meta information, as well as any other information being put together in a package such as a mpg, mov, avi, etc. Each part or stream may be compressed so that it uses up less space. The final size of the video is determined by the quality of the video (the higher number of bits per second, the better the quality), audio (same thing), the quality of the compression method, and the length of the recording. The way compressing and decompressing data in media streams is handled by a set of instructions called a "codec." Codec stands for compression - decompression. This set of instructions is also known as software, and in some cases, malicious instructions are added to this software. This is why people get infected after they visit porn sites that instruct them to download a codec in order to watch their smut. Codecs as well as full software applications are needed to convert from one file format to another. This section list various conversion applications, codecs, and other applications needed to view and convert between various video formats. The process of converting from one format to another is called, "transcoding." Almost every media producer at one time or another has had to transcode their media from one format to another.

VLC Media Player

VLC Media player is a video player that works on many different operating systems such as Linux, MacOS, Windows, BSD, and more. It can be obtained by visiting http://www.videolan.org/vlc/. Using a computer with Windows XP installed, the author was dismayed that the computer would not play a movie DVD without being prompted to purchase a codec. The author expected Windows Media Player to be able to handle the job since it was after all, a media player. Instead of buying a codec or other expensive media software, the author downloaded VLC Media Player. This feature rich software can handle playing not only regular DVD's as well as Hollywood produced DVD's, but it can also play video files in 3gp, avi, asf, mpg, mp4, mov, ogg, ogm, wav, wma, wmv, and a few more. It can also handle subtitles and on some platforms, closed captioning as well.

FFmpeg

FFmpeg is an ultra powerful command line format conversion software package. It is available for Windows, Linux, MacOS, BSD, and other platforms. FFmpeg's strengths is the fact that it can convert from most file formats to other file formats. Unfortunately, since it is command line driven, users have to spend time learning how to use the software as far as learning what parameters to use to get the package to do what they want it to do. Fortunately, there are plenty of FFmpeg tutorials and sample uses available on-line. FFmpeg is great for people who do batch transcoding and write their own scripts. FFmpeg is one of the author's favorite video production tools.

HandBrake

Handbrake is a video converter and transcoder available for Windows, Linux, MacOS, and BSD. Handbrake is available by visiting http://handbrake.fr/.

DVD Authoring

There is a difference between data DVD's and video DVD's. People will try to copy their video files to a DVD and expect it to play in a standard DVD player only to find a message stating that a DVD video is not found.

Many people try to just copy the video they produce to their DVD's and find that their DVD will not play in many standard DVD players. Some DVD players, however, will play video files that are burned to data DVD's. However, this is an extra feature found on some DVD players, but it is not a guarantee for most standard DVD players. For a DVD to be played on most standard DVD players require that the DVD to be authored. Authoring a DVD entails converting video files to a format that the DVD player understands as well as providing the DVD player instructions on how to display menus, titles, and other information. DVD authoring involves the use of DVD authoring software. There are many DVD authoring programs with various features and qualities that can be found on-line. Some of these will be mentioned later in this chapter.

DVD Media Types

Another factor involved in creating video DVD's that will play in most DVD players is the type of blank DVD's purchased. There are DVD-R, DVD+R, DVD-RW, and DVD+RW. These are all different and relate to how information is actually burnt onto the recording surface. DVD-R is the type of blank DVD that is compatible with most players out there. DVD-RW is the next compatible type of blank DVD. The suffix after the minus or plus sign indicated whether the blank can be written only once or if it can be written many times. The suffix "R" indicates that the DVD can be written only once while the suffix "RW" indicated that it can be written multiple times.

Another factor that important in DVD compatibility is the speed at which the DVD is written. The slower the burn speed, the more DVD playing devices that will successfully play the DVD.

Animated Loops

Another thing that should be mentioned when producing video DVD is that video DVD's can be given a professional edge by using animated backgrounds or loops. Animated backgrounds are displayed behind any menu items on the DVD menu screen. Hollywood producers use animated backgrounds to give their products additional flair. Example of

such animated backgrounds can be found at
http://www.movietools.info.

Bombono

The Bombono DVD authoring program is one of the author's favorite DVD authoring program. It allows both text based and image based menus, animated menu items, animated background, and also subtitles. With the Linux version of the software, all of these features come free. However, at the time of this writing, the full featured version for Windows is available as a thirty day trial or for purchase at the price of $24.95.

DVD Styler

DVD Styler is another program that is available for Linux, BSD, Mac OSX, and Windows. DVD Styler, while not as feature rich as Bombono, is still a great program for authoring home and semi-professional DVD's.

DVD Flick

DVD Flick is another very good DVD authoring program that is available for Microsoft Windows. DVD Flick provides many different features such as subtitles, customizable template, ability to convert over forty file formats to DVD playable format and many others. DVD Flick is available for downloading by visiting http://www.dvdflick.net/index.php.

Screen Capturing and Recording

Many how to videos show programs in actual use. Rather than using a camera to record what is happening on the computer's screen, most producers use a desktop recording application to get the job done. Some of the screen recording programs are free and open source. Two of these include CamStudio and recordMyDesktop. CamStudio is available for the Windows operating system and can be downloaded by visiting http://www.camstudio.org. CamStudio even allows users to add captions and annotations to their recordings.

RecordMyDesktop. RecordMyDesktop is available for both Linux and BSD.
RecordMy Desktop can be downloaded by visiting http://recordmydesktop.sourceforge.net.
Mac OSX users can use the Quicktime program in order to make desktop recordings. Unfortunately, at the time of this writing, there are very few free screen recording options for Mac OSX.

Distribution

Videos can be distributed in many different ways. These include distribution over video sharing sites, via DVD's, to streaming video devices, and through video download websites. It is recommended that several modes of distribution be used for each title. This is due to the fact that many people may use their smart phones to watch video instead of a DVD player. Others may use a DVD player and may not even have a cell phone. Making video available in different formats enable a wider audience to be able to watch. The fewer people left out, the wider the audience.

Chapter 5
Publishing Print Material

Authoring a book is a challenge, and it can also be fun. This author has published a book, and in doing so, has learned much. Some of the trick of the trade is offered in this chapter. For the self published author, much of the work such as editing, formatting, cover art, and file conversion has to be done by the author his or her self or be contracted to others. The more that the author does, the less money the author will have to invest in his or her publication. Fortunately, with the advent of the Internet, there are plenty of websites that provide clip art that can be used in cover design. These too will be listed in this chapter.

There are many people who talk about writing books, and although there are a myriad of books out there, only a relatively small percentage of the population write them. The people who do spend the time writing a book usually devote quite a bit of their time and resources into doing so. Many have hear about the horror stories of submissions, rejection letters, typed manuscripts, agent fees, and so on. These are come of the pitfalls that many first time authors fall into. First, is the fact that the publishing business has changed. This means that typewritten manuscripts for the most part are out. We now live in the information age, and most publishing or book printing firms expect the work to be in some sort of digital format. Another pitfall that first time authors may fall into is being used by the vanity presses. Instead of expecting to make money from book sales, vanity presses expect to make money from authors. This means that they will publish any kind of drivel if paid the right price. If an author decides against using a tradition publisher where his or her work is likely to be rejected, there is another option, and that option is one of the book printing services out there.

When going it alone, the author must take on several tasks when it comes to the design of his or her book. This includes not only writing the content, but also the mechanical design of the book itself. The mechanical design includes figuring out the trim size, the page format of the book, indexing, cover art, etc. Trim size is the final size of the pages of the book after the excess edges have been cut off. Self published authors must make sure that there is bleed to the maximum edge of the page before trim. This is especially true for cover designs. When designing a book to be sold through various outlets, the author or publisher must be aware of the standards used in book industry. Books that fail to comply with these standards will be rejected out of hand for distribution to most stores. The industry standard paperback book sizes (in inches) are 5" x 8", 5.06" x 7.81", 5.25" x 8", 5.5" x 8.5", 6" x 9", 6.14" x 9.21", 6.69" x 9.61", 7" x 10", 7.44" x 9.69", 7.5" x 9.25", 8" x 10", and 8.5" x 11". Another requirement for books to be sold in most stores is the presence of an International Standard Book Number or ISBN. This number and bar code is unique to each title, edition, and style. A hard cover book of the same title will have a different ISBN than the paperback edition, and the large print edition will also have a different ISBN.

All of this is a lot of information to process and comprehend. Fortunately, there is a company out there whose business is to help self published authors get their work printed. This company is called, "Create Space."

Create Space has a number of tools, template, and utilities that make the job of the self published author much easier. The best part is the fact that these tools are free for the author to use. The royalty calculator will show the author how much he or she can make from each book. The book cover graphics template will guide the author in the size of his or her cover design graphic. Formatting templates helps the author remain with guidelines for page formatting. All of these tools help the self published author. Create Space requires the interior files to be submitted in a PDF format. The book cover is also required to be submitted as a pdf document.

Create Space provides instructions on how to do all of this with Microsoft Office and Adobe's Photoshop, but not for G.I.M.P. or other free software. It's not too difficult to do, however. As far as the interior of the book goes, all one has to do is download Create Space's Open Office book templates and use it to enter text for the interior. As far as the book cover is concerned, a graphic

template is provided as well. One can then use their graphics program to select, copy,
and then paste the usable part of the template into one's favorite graphics editing program (The author recommends G.I.M.P.). The template markings can be removed as the cover graphics is being done. After the cover graphics is complete, the file should be saved as a png file. Open Office Draw can be opened and using the Format menu item, the page can be selected, all margins removed, and the page size set according to Create Space's specifications. After that is done, the graphics file for the cover can be inserted and then the entire thing can finally be saved as a pdf file.

One of the best ways to write a book is to use a simple text editor to create the manuscript and then copy and paste the entire thing into Open Office after the book template has been opened. This will allow the the writer to create his or her work and not be distracted by worrying about all of the formatting. In addition, using a simple text editor will also allow the writer to save the final manuscript as a text file where it can be inserted or pasted into Open Office Writer as well as an html editor (so that it can be converted to an e-book edition as well).

PosteRazor

A good yet free program for printing temporary posters or signs is a program called, "PosteRazor." PosteRazor is available for Windows, Linux, and Mac OSX. This program will allow someone to open a jpg graphics file and then have PosteRazor covert the file into several pdf pages. These pdf files are then printed individually, trimmed, and then taped together in order to make the poster. This is a great way to make temporary signs or promotional material. PosteRazor can be obtained by visiting, http://posterazor.sourceforge.net.

Open Office

Open Office is much more than a word processor. It is an entire office suite that is compatible with Microsoft Office. Microsoft Office has Word while Open Office has Writer. Both do the same thing. Microsoft Office has Power Point while Open Office has Presenter. Both of these do the same thing as well. Microsoft Office has Photo Edit while Open Office has draw. Yet again, both of these do the same thing. In fact most Microsoft Office files can be opened, edited, and saved using Open Office. Open Office as well as it offshoots (Libre Office) run in Windows, Linux, Mac OSX, BSD, and other platforms. Open Office can be downloaded by visiting http://www.openoffice.org.

G.I.M.P.

G.I.M.P. is a graphics editing package with most of the same features as the expensive Adobe Photoshop application. Despite its name, G.I.M.P. is not limited featured cripple ware. It is a very capable graphics editing suite with many different features and effects. Although it may not have every bell and whistle as Photoshop, it has enough to be a very powerful application in its own right. The best part about G.I.M.P. is the fact that it is totally free. It can be used to draw free hand, it can also be used to add effects. G.I.M.P. is available by visiting http://www.gimp.org. It is available for Windows, Linux, Mac OSX, and BSD.

E-books

E-books are another way of distributing printed or text material on-line. There are several popular e-book file formats. These include mobi, epub, html, pdf as well as many others. At the time of this writing, the mobi format is the most universal being able to be read on just about any e-book reader or reader application. Many people choose to create pdf files since pdf software is widely installed on computers and is used for many on-line, published documents. While pdf files may be fine for computers and for printing said documents on paper, they are a poor choice to use as a format for e-book readers. This is due to the fact that it is difficult to re-flow text so that it fits the smaller screens of e-book reading devices. When publishing an e-book, one should pay close attention to the terms and conditions of any site where such a book is to be published. This is due to the fact that some user agreements stipulated that the user give up all ownership of the material to be published. That means the owner of the site can claim the work as his or her own and in some cases, keep the creator from publishing elsewhere.

E-books can be distributed on-line is several different ways. They can be posted as files to websites, distributed via peer to peer networking, emailed directly to e-book reader devices, and uploaded to one of the several e-book sites. The advantages and disadvantages of each are noted.

There are several advantages to posting e-books on an independent website. Advantages include being able to have a page that allows the user to choose the file format of the e-book, being able to log information about the user's visit such as the type of e-reader used, the location of the reader, and the ability to embed dynamic content into the e-book tailored to that specific user. Another advantage, if uploading to one of the many e-book websites is the ability of having relatively good anonymity. Disadvantages include the fact that certain e-readers may not be configured to access the site where the book is hosted, the cost of running the website, and the cost of promoting the website to reach users. There is also the disadvantage of having to set up a payment system in order to collect money from customers if the e-book is for sale.

E-books can also be distributed over file sharing networks. This allows the original distributor to be relatively anonymous if done correctly. Being able to distribute e-books in this format is an advantage when the contents of said books happen to violate the sensibilities or rules of government authorities or powerful organizations such as illegal drug cartels. There are disadvantages as well. One of the disadvantages is the fact that it is nearly impossible to stop the distribution once it starts especially if the book is popular. Another disadvantage is the inability to collect or enforce copyright protections.

Using electronic mail or email to distribute books is another way of electronic publishing. Using email allows one to connect to the Internet, send the book, and disconnect. Depending how the user connects to the Internet as well as the type of email address used by the user, it can also provide a high degree on anonymity. However, there are disadvantages as well. One disadvantage is the fact that the publisher will have to set up his or her own system for collecting payments of the published work is sold. Another disadvantage is the fact that accounts with the e-book reader manufacturer must be configured to allow files and email from the publisher's publishing address to be downloaded to the e-book reading device. E-book reader manufacturers usually block everything that is sent to the email address to which the e-book reader is linked in order to prevent spamming.

Another way to distribute e-books is through the websites of e-book reader manufacturers. For example, the Amazon Kindle is produced by Amazon (or it contractors). Amazon has a website that allows authors to publish electronic books for the Kindle device. This website is http://kdp.amazon.com. The Nook, which is produced by Barnes and Noble also has a website dedicated to authors who wish to sell or give away e-books. This website is http://www.bn.com/pubit. These two site provide publishing for most of the e-book reading devices out there. The advantage to using the e-book reader website is the fact that the e-book reader is already configured to download books from these sites. They also include payment processing and handling. One disadvantage to such site is that they require personal information such as name, "Social Security" number, address, and banking information. Another disadvantage to such a site is the fact that they can and have censored books that go against government rules.

Anybody who publishes their own literature would be very wise to publish an electronic edition as well. In fact, many authors make more money by selling electronic books than the do the printed version. The best part about releasing an e-book is the fact that it cost next to nothing to do so. The book has to be written and converted to a format that the e-reader can handle. There are different free programs that can handle this task. They are also listed in this chapter.

Calibre

Calibre is an eabook reader, ebook conversion program, and an e-book collections manager. Calibre is available for Linux, Windows, and Mac OSX. It can open cbz, cbr, cbc, chm, djvu, epub, fb2, html, htmlz, lit, lrf, mobi, odt, pdf, prc, pdb, pml, rb, rtf, snb, tcr, txt, and txtz. It can covert any file it can open to epub, fb2, oeb, lit, lrf, mobi, htmlz, pdb, pml, rb, pdf, rtf, snb, tcr, txt, and txtz.

Sigil

Sigil is another e-book program. The main output for Sigil is the epub format since it is primarily an epub editor. Sigil is available for Linux, Windowss and Mac OSX and can be downloaded by visiting http://code.google.com/p/sigil/.

Scribus

Scribus is a publishing program that assists with document layouts. It is not a word processor and doesn't act like one. As the user manual says, it is used in the final assembly of a published work. What this means is that one cannot just create a new document and start typing right away without knowing how to provide at least some information. Scribus takes some time to learn, but it is a worthwhile program to learn how to use. For example, one can use Scribus to publish a book, but in doing so, it would be best to search the Internet for terms such as "how to produce a book using Scribus." Even though the author has not used Scribus to create or publish a book, Scribus is another free option to expensive software. Scribus can be downloaded by visiting http://www.scribus.net/. Scribus work with Linux, Windows, Mac OSX, and BSD.

Optical Character Recognition

Optical character recognition (OCR) is the process of taking printed media or graphics files and converting text contained within into character or text data. Old, out of print books can be scanned with an inexpensive scanner, and the resulting graphics file can be fed into an OCR program. The resulting text is likely to contain errors, but these can be corrected. Another way to use such a program is use a screen capture program and then run the resulting graphics file through the OCR program and get the text output. This is good for programs where copy and pasts functions have been disabled.

Tesseract OCR

Tesseract is available for Linux, and versions are also available for Windows. The Linux version is available by visiting http://code.google.com/p/tesseract-ocr/ or by using distribution specific package manager. The Windows version can be downloaded by visiting http://www.paperfile.net/.

GOCR

GOCR is another OCR program available for Linux. It is also known as JOCR It is available for download by visiting http://jocr.sourceforge.net/download.html or by using distribution specific package manager.

Online OCR

An online tool that performs optical character recognition can be found at http://www.free-ocr.com/. Another on-line tool that can perform the same task can be found at http://www.newocr.com/. The good part about using on-line tools is the fact that they can be used with tablet computers without taking up precious space for programs.

This chapter explains the various programs and tools needed to publish text material. It explains different methods of obtaining text. Distribution methods are also explained.

Chapter 6
Internet Production and Publishing

One of the ways of reaching the largest potential audience for the least amount of money is by the use of the Internet. The Internet gives anybody with a decent connection a platform. As said before, the Internet is the greatest media tool since the printing press. It has the potential of making television, radio, and print media nearly obsolete. Therefore, Internet publishing should at least have a mention in this book, and it does.

Even though we are in the Twenty First Century, there are many businesses that do not have their own website yet. This also presents an opportunity for the content creator. In addition, the content creator can also create new webpages in order to promote his or her products. Another use for web pages is to provide informational articles that are embedded with advertising. If one of these web pages becomes widely visited by people, embedded advertising revenue may add up. Another use is for the webpage designer to embed advertising related to his or her music, videos, or books.

Webpages are simply information on the world wide web that people view using their web browsers. Webpages in their most basic form consists of HTML (hyper text markup language) or XHTML (Extensible hyper text markup Language) and may include other files such as CSS (cascading style sheets), graphics, audio, video, applets, scripts, or applications. Most basic web publishing programs while they allow the use or embedding of audio, video, applets, scripts, or applications, are primarily designed to produce HTML code. With a couple of days of time devoting to learning HTML, one can use a basic word processor and create web pages that load quickly and look good. One can also use many of the free (and paid) web page publication programs out there as well.

Setting up a website involves a few steps. One of the first things that is required is to register a domain. A domain is one's Internet name that is used to pull up a site. Domain names includes google.com, plaza1.net, freelink.cx, etc. Domain names can be purchased from many different registrars. A registrar is a company that sells domain name space to people. After a domain name is registered, a hosting service needs to be found. Hosting services can be found for anywhere from a few dollars per month up to thousands depending upon the needs of the website owner. Some popular hosting providers also provide templates or patterns, so to speak, that can be used to design websites. These allow people to quickly put together a good looking site. Other services just provide space on a computer to which webpages can be uploaded. One thing that must be pointed out is that there are free web hosting services out there. These free services usually embed advertising banners throughout the page. Webpages hosted on such free services usually look unprofessional due to the number of advertising banners embedded. This section lists different domain registrars as well as web hosting services. After a domain name is registered and a hosting service is found, the next step is to design a web site.

If the web hosting provider provides template

that the user desires to use, then he or she can design the website using these provider-based tools and follow the providers instructions for publishing the site. If the designer wishes to use his or her own web design program or text editor to put together the site, then he or she will need to upload the resulting files to the hosting service. This is usually done with the file transfer protocol (FTP), secure file transfer protocol, or in some cases via a web interface provided by the hosting service. Most operating systems either provide the ftp or sftp program as a command line program. One can also download one of the many free ftp programs on-line.

Websites that embed video, audio, and other multimedia content often require high bandwidth for each person that visits. Bandwidth is the amount of data that can be transmitted at a period of time. Some web hosting services will set a specific amount of data (bytes megabytes or gigabytes) that can be used each month. Any usage over the limit is either forbidden or will incur extra charges. One way to save money when using such hosting services is to upload the multimedia portion of the page to a free service such as

You Tube and then embed a link to the content on the hosted website.

The Languages of the Web

Hypertext markup language, or HTML is the basic language of the World Wide Web. HTML is a simple language that tells web browsers how to display text, images, videos, and other content. HTML consists of tags, attributes, and text. It can also contain embedded script such as Visual Basic Script or the more commonly used Javascript. HTML is a very simple language that can be learned in under a week by anyone with enough discipline to spend an hour or two reading per day. A website, http://www.w3schools.com/html/ provides a free tutorial on how to learn HTML. It is highly recommended that anyone who builds websites regularly to learn HTML. It is not that hard to learn. For those who do not want to take the time to learn html can use a web designer program to build their site. A few free programs for doing this will be discussed at the end of this section. There are some other files that can enhance the display of a webpage or website. These are discussed in the next few paragraphs.

Cascading Style Sheets

One commonly used file that enhances the display of a webpage is called the Cascading Style Sheet or CSS. The cascading style sheet allows a particular set of text styles to be shared across many different HTML files on a website. Using a cascading style sheet file is advantageous due to the fact that a font size, color, or any other attribute can be made to a single file instead of having to go through the laborious task of changing each HTML file on the site. Learning how to use and make cascading style sheets will make the life of a web designer much easier. To learn CSS, one can visit http://www.w3schools.com/css/. This too is a free tutorial.

Javascript

Another common type of file is the Javascript file. It commonly has the extension .js. Javascript can be used to create very stunning effects as well as allowing a webpage to function as an application. Javascript is harder to learn than either HTML or CSS. Javascript is not the same as Java which is yet another computer language that can be used to enhance webpages. Javascript can be learned by visiting http://www.w3schools.com/js/.

Flash and Actionscript

Flash applications also play an important part of the World Wide Web. Flash is a proprietary language developed by Macromedia. Macromedia was bought by Adobe, however. Flash is in and of itself a proprietary platform. The language that is used to develop Flash programs is called Action Script. Flash development can be learned by visiting http://www.echoecho.com/flash.htm as well as many other pages. Most development of Flash applications (or movies) is done by using Adobe's expensive program called, Flash Professional CS. However, the good news is the fact that hackers have designed open source Flash development tools some of which include http://www.mtasc.org/.

Java

One other commonly used language for developing cross platform applications as well as applets used on webpages is Java. Java was created by the people at Sun. Sun was bought by Oracle which currently maintains the Java language. Java can be learned by visiting http://docs.oracle.com/javase/tutorial/java/index.html. Not only is Oracle's Java Development Kit free for downloading, but there are also other, open source, Java development platforms out there. The author sticks with Oracle's platform since it is free to download and use.

The languages listed in this section range from easy to learn (HTML and CSS) to those as complex as Flash ActionScript and Java. For the beginning web site developer, it is highly recommended that he or she learn at least HTML and CSS. These two relatively easy to learn languages can be used to create great looking websites. For those who do not want to bother learning these two languages or are too lazy or pressed for time to write code from scratch, there are several webpage creation programs or editors that can be used to speed the task. Here are a few:

Kompozer

Kompozer is a relatively easy to use web page editor that is available for Mac OSX, Windows, and Linux. Kompozer is relatively easy to learn and includes basic features such as drag and drop feaures, easy text entry, tabbed editing, reliable html code generation, and support for form, tables, and templates. It can be downloaded by visiting http://kompozer.net/.

Openbexi

Openbexi is a "what you see is what you get" website designer program. Openbexi does have a steep learning curve. Tutorials are available to learn this application online. Openbexi is available for Linux, Mac OSX and Windows. Openbexi is available by visiting http://www.openbexi.com/.

Open Office

OpenOffice also has a function that allows users to export their creations as html files. This method is not an ideal solution, but it will work. Openoffice is available by visiting http://www.openoffice.org.

Domain Registrars

A domain registrar is an agency or company that allows people to purchase a domain name for a period of time. There are literally thousands of domain registrars, and the list presented in this book only covers the very popular ones.

Some companies offer both domain registration and hosting services. If deciding to use a company that provides both services, it is advisable to be very careful about using the same company to provide both of these services. This is due to the fact that if there is a billing dispute or other problem, a domain name cannot be held hostage by the host provider. Using separate services to host websites and register domains allow a customer to be able to quickly switch from one hosting provider to another in the event of dissatisfaction or billing dispute.

1and1.com

http://1and1.com not only offers domain registration at a very inexpensive price, but it also offers hosting services as well. 1And1 also offers private registration as well. This helps protect registrants' information from the prying eyes of spammers and other criminals.

Godaddy.com

http://www.godaddy.com is another very popular domain registration service. Like 1and1, Go Daddy also offers web hosting services. One thing about Go Daddy that potential customers need to be aware of is that Go Daddy uses up-selling tactics intended to entice customers into purchasing additional services. This is done through pop up messages and having such options already check marked. Customers should check each part of the registration process in order to make sure that these optional services are not selected before going on to the next step unless such add-ons are desired.

Another thing that customers should be aware of is the fact that after domain names expire, Go Daddy puts them up for auction. This means that if a customer allows his or her domain name to expire, then he or she may have to place bids on their domain name in order to get it back. This can get very expensive. Go Daddy also offers private registration as well for an additional price.

Name.com

Name is another registration service that offers domains for many different top level domains such as .com .net .cc, etc. Prices for domain names are relatively inexpensive at the time this is written. Name.com can be visited by going to http://www.name.com.

Namecheap.com

Namecheap is yet another inexpensive service that allows people to register domain names. Namecheap

Hosting Services

Hosting services are the companies that actually have the computers and network infrastructure to store and deliver web content to users. The good thing about the Internet is the fact that people all over the world can choose which company they want to use for Internet hosting regardless of the location of the hosting service or the client.

Hosting providers can offer a range of services from websites, chat services, Voice over IP, user created background processes, email addresses, as well as many more. For people who want to do all of these things, they can choose to have their own dedicated server. This can be either a virtual server where a single computer may host one or more other servers that each appear as though they are a separate computer, or they may choose having a dedicated server where each customer leases his or her own computer at the hosting provider's data center.

This means that not only can customers choose the prices and taxes that they are willing to pay, but they can also choose which legal jurisdiction they want in order to protect the content they wish to deliver. Some countries offer a wide range of protection for privacy, intellectual property, and free speech. Other places do not offer the same level of protection in each area. Therefore, it is up to the producer or publisher to choose a web hosting option that is ideal for his or her situation. In cases where a publisher is dissatisfied with the quality of service, he or she can switch providers. This is usually not a problem especially when different companies are used to register the publisher's domain and host the website. Just because a company is listed in this book does not mean that the author specifically endorses the company or its business practices. The author chooses to list just some of the most popular services.

1and1.com

1and1 offers all kinds of different hosting option starting at less than five dollars a month at the time this is written to almost four hundred dollars per month for hosting company networks. 1and1 comes with a wide range of tools and web and application design templates for most needs and skill levels. The author considers 1and1 hosting one of the best out there. Another reason 1and1 hosting is so good is due to the fact that this company allows customers to set up their own services such as Voice over IP (Internet telephony), chat servers, etc. One can look at the many different options offered by 1and1 Internet services simply by visiting http://www.1and1.com.

Godaddy.com

Go Daddy is another web hosting company that offers different options depending upon the publisher or producer's needs. Go Daddy offers many different inexpensive hosting solutions some of which run less than ten dollars per month for unlimited bandwidth. Go Daddy can be evaluated by visiting http://www.godaddy.com.

Hostgator.com

The last hosting site example listed here is Host Gator. This service offers many different options in addition to web hosting.

These include a SSL (Secure Sockets Layer) certificate which allows customers to view website using a sceure connection without the viewer's web browser complaining that the security certificate is not authentic. Host Gator also allows the use of quite a number of email addresses. The included number depends upon the hosting plan chosen. Customers can go to http://www.hostgator.com for more information.

Video Sharing Sites

There are plenty of video sharing site where one can show his or her video. Each has its advantages and disadvantages. Some of these sites as well as their advantages and disadvantages are listed below. Some of these sites require the user to upload videos in specific formats while others allow more choices in the formats used. It is recommended that producers of video upload to at least two of the sites listed below in order to reach as many devices and audience members as possible. Some streaming devices will not work with a certain site while it will work fine on another. One may wonder why android phones and Apple iPads are not listed as streaming video devices. They are not listed because these devices have apps or applications that can be downloaded in order to play content from the websites listed. The websites listed in this section are some of the most popular.

Blip TV

Blip is a platform for high-quality web series and also offers a dashboard for producers of original web series to distribute and monetize their productions. Blip TV is for producers of video series and not for one time recordings. Blip TV accepts videos in H.264 m4v and flv formats. Blip works with streaming video devices such as Apple TV, Logitech Revue, and Roku. Blip TV only list the top few web series on their destination site. There is a one gigabyte limit on each video file uploaded. One can visit Blip TV by going to http://www.blip.tv.

Dailymotion

Dailymotion is a video sharing service that

ranks second to that of You Tube. Dailymotion allows users to browse and upload videos by searching tags, channels or user created groups. Dailymotion has three categories of users. These include regular users, motion maker users, and official users. Regular users are those who create accounts and have the ability to upload videos.

However regular users are limited to two gigabytes of file size and only at a resolution of up to 512 x 384 pixels. If a user wants to upload videos of unlimited file size, they can request to be upgraded to a motion maker category. Motion maker accounts are for those who produce original videos. At the time this is written, morion maker accounts are also free. Motion maker users are able to upload videos of a resolution of up to 1280×720 pixels and unlimited length. Official users are those with accounts registered as representing organizations, political campaigns, or companies. They have the same benefits as motion maker users.

Dailymotion supports mp4, wmv, mpeg, avi, dv, 3gp, and flv video formats. Dailymotion works on Apple TV devices only if they are jail broken (hacked to extend capabilities), Logitech Revue, and Roku. One can visit

Dailymotion by going to http://www.dailymotion.com.

Metacafe

Metacafe is a video site that specializes in short-form video entertainment in the categories of movies, video games, sports, music and TV. Much of the content featured on the home page are trailers or samples of entertainment industry's work. However, full featured videos can be uploaded, and resolutions up to 1920 x 1080 pixels are supported. Metacafe supports mpeg, mpg, mpe, avi, wmv, wmf, asf, m1v, divx, mov, mp4, flv, 3gp, rm, rmvb, rv, ram and mkv video formats. There is an eight minute limit on the length of the video. Metacafe works with the Logitech Revue streaming device. One can visit Metacafe by going to http://www.metacafe.com.

MySpaceTV

Myspace allows registered users to upload up to 100 megabytes of video. Myspace is useful only for very short informational or promotional clips. Myspace accepts asf, avi, divx, mkv, m1v, mov, mpeg, mpg, mpe, mp4, flv, 3gp, rm, rmvb, rv, ram, wmv, and wmf video formats.

Vimeo

Vimeo is a multipurpose video sharing website that offers both free and paid accounts. The free account allows a maximum of five hundred megabytes of file uploading per week. Paid accounts allow five gigabytes of file uploads per week which is ten times the quantity of the free account. At the time of this writing, the paid accounts costs just under sixty dollars. The pro account costs just under two hundred dollars per year and comes with a fifty gigabyte upload allowance per year and a 5 gigabyte individual file limit. Vimeo does not allow basic and plus accounts to upload videos promoting products or services. Vimeo accepts the mp4 video format and supports resolutions 640x480 pixels for standard definition and 1280 x 720 pixels for high definition. Vimeo also works with Roku.

You Tube

The biggest video sharing site is You Tube. You Tube has the advantage of being widely known. However, there is the disadvantage of having to put up with the restriction of video length. This can be overcome by splitting long videos into clips of less than fifteen minutes each. Users can remove the limit on the length of the video by clicking on a "increase limit" link and providing a cell phone number. This link will not show if a user has any unexpired copyright strikes or unexpired community guidelines violations. Another advantage to using You Tube to host a video is the fact that the video can still be embedded on another webpage and still be streamed from You Tube. You Tube also has a feature that allows a video to be unlisted so that viewers would have to have the exact URL to view the video.

Music Distribution Sites

Musicians also have plenty of choices when it comes to promoting and selling their music. Many different sites exist that allow musicians to both give away their music and sell it. In addition, those who want to release promotional tracks can, like other media producers, share some of their music on one of the many peer to peer file sharing sites. Other sites exists that allow musicians to sell their music as well. Some of the more popular ones are listed in this section.

Amazon Music

Amazon is one of the easiest places where an independent artist can sell music. This is probably one of the main reason why Amazon has become so successful. Amazon allows music creators to set the price of their music and also not only handles electronic distribution, but also CD's. Amazon allows music creators to submit their content through one of its subsidiaries, Create Space. To get started, all one has to do is visit http://www.createspace.com.

Paid Music Aggregator Services

There are plenty of paid music download sites where music can be sold by independent artists and publishers. Unfortunately, many of these site do not accept music directly from artists. This is where one of the many paid music distribution services come into play In order for music to appear on emusic.com, Rhapsody, Zune, and many others, the producer or artist must go through a third party site such as those listed below:

CD Baby (http://members.cdbaby.com/)
Tunecore (http://www.tunecore.com/)
Nimbit (http://www.nimbit.com)
Emu Bands (http://www.emubands.com/)

iTunes

iTunes is an electronic media store owned by Apple. This store offers distribution options not only for music but also video, books, and other media. The process of selling directly through iTunes is tedious, and one must meet many archaic requirement such as having an Apple computer, many items for sale, requisite product id numbers, etc. Even then, it is not really guaranteed that one will still be able to sell directly through this outfit. The author recommends using either an approved iTunes content aggregator or one of the paid distributions services discussed earlier in this section. For those who feel that they are willing to try anyway, a visit to http://www.apple.com/itunes/sellcontent/ is the starting point.

Pandora.com

Pandora is an Internet Radio service that allows users to create their own stations in order to play the music that they like to hear. Pandora does allow artists to directly submit their work, but it does have a few requirements. One must have a CD of their work, and that CD must have its own UPC, the CD must be available through Amazon, a Pandora account (can be the free one), and mp3 files of two tracks from the CD.
If one can meet these requirements, then he or she can head over to http://submit.pandora.com/ to get started.

Last Fm

Last.fm is yet another Internet radio service. Last.fm has relatively lax requirements for Artists to submit their works. In order to do this, an artist simply creates a (free) user account and then adds an artist or label account (also free). He or she will then be able to upload music. Last FM can be visited by going to http://www.last.fm.

Spotify

Spotify is yet another music streaming service. Getting an artists music onto Spotify requires the use of an aggregator service such as one listed earlier in this section. To learn about Spotify, one should visit http://www.spotify.com.

The You Tube Option

One of the most popular routes for artists to get their music on-line is to create a video, or combine a picture of the band with the audio track. Doing this results in a video file that shows this picture, or pictures while playing the sound track. This is perhaps one of the simplest and most inexpensive ways for an artist to promote themselves on-line. It is fairly simple to set up a You Tube account. One simply has to visit http://www.youtube.com and register a new account.

Transferring Files to a Website or Host

Once a hosting service or site to host content is selected. The files will then have to be uploaded to the site. There are two main ways of doing this, and these two ways are web based and the use of the File Transfer Protocol (FTP).

The web based method is usually specific to the provider hosting the site. Instructions for uploading in these cases are provided by the web hosting provider itself.

The usual second method of file transfer is usually accomplished by FTP or SFTP (Secure File Transfer Protocol). One program that provides this capability and more is called Filezilla. Filezilla is available by visiting http://filezilla-project.org.

A Mozilla Firefox extension that provides FTP capability is FireFTP. FireFTP is available by visiting http://fireftp.mozdev.org.

Chapter 7
Idea's for Making Money

Near the beginning of this book, it was stated that the common person had very little chance of becoming rich or famous by publishing or producing his or her own work. However, there are still ways money can be made in the business. Everyday people need video, audio, or print records for many different purposes. The person gathering the information and recording the event can make a decent profit by producing and publishing the resulting media. The producer or publisher will have to discuss with the client on how the client wants the event published. Does he or she want it put on a video site such as You Tube? Does the client want a printed book with pictures or narration? What about CD's or DVD's of the event. Does the client want to send out all of the print media his or herself or is that to be the producer's or publisher's job? Each of these things represents value added to the service provided.

Bar and Bat Miztvah's

The Bar or Bat Miztvah is usually a very important time in the life of a young Jewish person.   It is the time when he or she celebrate coming of age as well as becoming a full member of the congregation. It is also an important time for the parents as this represents a significant milestone in their child's life. It is something most Jews who celebrate the occasion would want to have on record.   It also represents a way for the videographer to obtain work.

Church Services

Many people do not get to leave their homes. Others have found themselves in situations where they have had to move away from their hometowns.   Others may not like the churches in their area. Other congregations might want to use the information age to reach out to new people.   All of these situations represent an opportunity for a person to either volunteer or get paid to record, produce, and distribute audio, video, or both types of recording of church services.

Someone who does this can look at spending up to a couple of hours of time for each hour of recording in editing media, transcoding to proper formats, and uploading video recordings to the various video sites.

Working a Political Campaign

A person working a political campaign either for or against a candidate or encumbant has the ability to profit from the work in many ways. This profiting can be done by producing video, audio, print, or other material. For a small time producer or publisher, reaching out to local candidates will more likely bring in a contract rather than state or federal candidates. There are several ways of featuring a local candidate, and these include interviews, a candidate's good works in a community, or any other type of video where the candidate can be seen by others. Another side of the coin can also include producing a video showing a candidate's opponents in action. In cases where this is done, one should make sure that they use candid video or audio clips.

Domain Squatting

Domain squatting is done is by buying real estate - Internet real estate that is. In other words, a media publisher or producer can register domain names that contain the names of a company, person, or organization. For political elections, the time for doing this is not when a candidate announces his campaign but rather some time before. Registering domain names in anticipation of someone running for office is gambling. However, once someone is elected, it is time to anticipate desired domain names for that candidate's re-election even before he or she even takes office. This increases the odds of winning. If Dick Scott has just won the election, it's 2010, and Dick's term is four years, then it is a good idea to register dickscott2014.com, re-electdick.com as well as any variants that might be desired by encumbents or political action committees. If registration is kept current, then re-election time will most likely be very profitable or provide a powerful tool.

However, when registering a domain for a

high profile person, that domain should be set to point to a website, blog, etc that contains educational material about the person. This needs to be done in order to prevent trademark issues, etc. If the encumbent or political organization wants the domain, they can negotiate a price. Doing this is a tricky proposition since there are tort laws against a practice of domain squatting. Domain squatting is where a person registers a name or trademark belonging to another person with the hopes of selling that domain name to the person who owns the name or trademark or hopes to profit from the traffic generated by the name or trademark. Demonstrating an attempt to generate such profits is considered a tortuous action and can cause the registrant to not only lose the domain name, but also cause the registrant to be sued in court for large amounts of money. The way around this is to use such a domain name for a legitimate parody or gripe site. In doing so, one, when contacted by the trademark holder, MUST NOT offer to sell the domain to the owner nor have advertising or links to other site that can be construed to be advertising. Any such offer needs to be done by the name or trademark holder. This book is not about the legal or court system, and anyone who is considering such actions should study the law carefully or consult a lawyer.

Being a Stringer

A stringer is a freelance journalist who looks for stories and who record these stories while they happen. The stringer will then sell his or her recordings to various news outlets. They are usually paid for each individual work and are not salaried employees. Being a stringer may involve some risks especially if witnessing an event such as severe weather, crimes, or other emergency events. However, such risk also may bring rewards (financial) especially when the story is a big one and the stringer is the only one who happens to record the story.

Local Business Promotions

Video, audio, and print material can be produced for local consumption. Some of these videos can feature how to instructions or videos on local attractions or news. It can be, in effect, a local video magazine. Such videos can contain clips of local businesses and the products and services they offer. If more than one edition is produced, and businesses receive feedback from the video's viewers, they may be inclined to pay to be included in future editions. An example of one type of video that can be produced is one called how to move to the Panama City, Florida area. A video like this can discuss what is needed to be done to get a Florida's drivers license, what permits are required to set up a home, zoning rules to be aware of, and when to avoid certain areas due to crime, traffic, enforcement, etc. Local businesses may consider paying to be included in a local "Things to See and Do" section.

Selling Media On-line

Books, video, and audio productions can be sold in physical forms on-line, or they can be sold as downloads. This book already discussed where to go and what to do in order to accomplish these tasks. When setting a price for content, one should consider the format in which the content is offered. For example, most people will think it is unfair for an electronic book to be priced at the same price as a paperback edition of the same book.

The creator of any work should decide his or her desired profit and calculate the price of the product by adding this profit, the cost of production, and the cost of distribution. An electronic download of a specific work costs less than making a physical book, CD, or DVD of the same, and the end price should reflect that.

Wedding Video's

People get married (and divorced) daily. In most cases, people getting married want a recording of the wedding and reception. This is where a a video producer can step in and offer his or her services. One of the best places to troll for potential clients are by have in a strong presence on social networking sites. People int his line of work should check out the profiles of local acquaintances. Another way is to take a look in the local newspaper (yes, people still read those) for wedding announcements.

There are plenty of ways to make money, and this chapter only lists a few. When someone wants to get an idea, entertainment, or other product out, there is a chance to make money.

Chapter 8
Promotion and Marketing

One of the hardest things a producer or publisher of content has to do is making people aware of their product as well as making them want to buy it. Some of the tricks used by the big companies and advertising firms include giveaways, repetition, and emotions. Most everyday people cannot afford to launch massive advertising campaigns on television, radio, or newspapers. Most cannot afford to give away many expensive items such as e-book readers, tablet computer, etc. However, most can publish advertisements on the Internet and locally, entertain, and appeal to people's emotions. These things alone are powerful tools.

Getting the Appropriate Numbers and Codes

One thing that those who produce and publish should know is that most stores and many Internet outlets will not sell items that do not have certain numbers and corresponding bar codes that are prescribed by standards. The kind of code that is assigned to an item depends upon what type of item is being sold.

Some production and publishing outfits such as Create Space provide authors and producers with a free ISBN or UPC. Companies that can do this rely on the fact that bulk purchases of these numbers are relative inexpensive compared to someone needing only a few of these numbers. Some number issuing organizations will charge a hefty (for small producers or publisher) annual membership fee and allow numbers to be purchased for a small additional expense. Others will charge a hefty fee for the first few numbers and a small fee per number for many additional ones. Each issuing agency is different, but their pricing scheme (of course) favor larger outfits. In addition to needing a number, one will also need the correct bar code which will allow the number to be inputted into the point of sale terminal (a.k.a. cash register). The software for making and reading bar codes will also be discussed.

There are advantages and disadvantages for buying one's own purchased numbers compared with using a production outfit or publisher assigned number. Using a company provided one means that all searches using that assigned number will point to the

company to which the number is assigned. That means that that company will decide how to handle or forward any resulting orders or requests. If the company assigning the number goes out of business, then that number is orphaned, and person who created the product for which the number is assigned will have to obtain another number from somewhere else. If one orders the number from the issuing organization directly, then he or she becomes the producer or publisher. It means that distributors will then order the product directly from that person. The producer or publisher will have to deal with taking orders, packaging the product, and then shipping the product. If an item takes off and becomes popular, that person will quickly become overwhelmed. Each of the number types will be discussed in this section.

Universal Product Code

An Universal Product Code or UPC is usually

assigned to general merchandise as well as many CD's or DVD's. These numbers are twelve digits and appear underneath the bar codes found on many different products. The organization which issues these numbers is GS1 US, a nonprofit group that sets standards for international commerce.

Companies pay to join GS1 US, and for their membership, they get a six digit id number which forms the first part of the UPC. They can then assign the next five digits of the UPC to individual products. The last digit will be a checksum digit. The website one can visit to obtain UPC numbers is http://www.gs1us.org/. Another website where individual UPC numbers can be very inexpensively purchased is http://www.nationwidebarcode.com/.

The International Standard Book Number

The International Standard Book Number or ISBN is assigned to media that is in physical book form as well as some electronic books. The modern numbers are thirteen digits in length, and the older numbers are ten digits in length. The first three digits of the ISBN will almost always be 978 or 979 with 978 being the most common. The next part is a group code. Then comes the publisher code. After that is the book title code. Finally, there is a single checksum digit. The ISBN is a necessary mark in order to sell a book in most chain or Internet stores. An ISBN can be purchased in the United States by visiting http://www.bowker.com/en-US/.

The International Standard Serial Number

The International Standard Serial Number or ISSN is assigned to printed or electronic periodical such as magazines. An ISSN is an anonymous identifier associated with a periodical title, containing no information as to the publisher or its location. The ISSN is a necessary mark in order to sell periodicals in most chain or Internet stores.
An ISSN can be obtained from the Library of Congress by visiting http://www.loc.gov/issn/issnbro.html.

Bar Codes

In addition to obtaining the correct number, a corresponding bar code will also need to be applied to the publication. The good new is the fact that there are plenty of free programs that both generate and read bar codes. The bar code generating programs listed in this section generate graphics files which can be copied and pasted onto the graphics files of book covers. Some publishing and printing outfits such as Create Space will generate these bar codes and place them for the author.

Barcode4J

Barcode4J is a program that runs on any operating system that has Java installed. This includes Linux, Windows, MacOS, BSD as well as many others. This program will generate bar codes for popular forms of media including UPC, ISBN (EAN-13), and ISSN (EAN-13). Barcode4Jv is available by visiting http://barcode4j.sourceforge.net/.

Zbar

Zbar is a program that identifies the bar code type as well as displaying the encoded information. Zbar has two separate programs that can read information from either a camera or from an image file. Zbar runs on

BSD, MAC OSX (via other sites), Linux, and Windows. It is available for download by visiting http://sourceforge.net/projects/zbar/.

Guerrilla Advertising

Guerrilla advertising involves using low cost and unconventional means of getting a message out. There are many ways of using this method. Some of them include leafleting, flash mobs, graffiti, sticker bombing, and many other ways. Some guerrilla marketing campaigns use unconventional techniques such a blue-jacking (spamming other users through bluetooth connections), printing on currency (illegal but usually overlooked), Hijacking signs, scrawling messages in dust or dirt, and many other ways. Guerrilla marketing are for those companies or individuals who don't have big advertisement budgets.

Social Media

Social media such as Facebook, Twitter, Pinterest, and many others are being used to harness the power of numbers. It has been used to elect a U.S. President, topple dictators, make grievances known to a wide number of people, expose atrocities, and to promote products and services. It now competes with big government and big money in inspiring millions to act. It is a very powerful tool in the right (or wrong) hands. The type of campaign that a middle class individual can run is much different than one that is run by a big company. That is because someone representing a big company can easily gain the audience of another big company and can also afford brand name giveaways. This is something that the average Joe working day to day cannot usually afford to do. The trick to making social media work is to come up with an innovative idea to get people interested, pique their curiosity, make them laugh, or otherwise invoke their emotions. Using emotions is the key of getting things to work. When one figures out how to strongly evoke people's emotions and then channel them towards (or against) a cause, product, service, or action, then most of the battle is complete. If that happens, people will do the work for the person who built the social networking campaign. Useful emotions for getting

138

people to click or act are curiosity, anger, greed, humor, love, and more.

A recent campaign started with single images, "KONY 2012." Variants showed, "KONY 2012 STOP AT NOTHING," "KONY 2012 MAKE HIM FAMOUS," "KONY 2012 MAKE HIM VISIBLE," and an image showing the Democratic Party's logo and the Republican party logo merging with the words, "KONY 2012 ONE THING WE CAN ALL AGREE ON" printed in the foreground. There was not much other detail, but there was enough information on these images to evoke the emotion of curiosity. "KONY 2012" looked very much like an election campaign image, and in an election year, it was enough to get some people to find information about a candidate they have never heard about. This curiosity manipulated them into visiting a website where there was more information as well as an emotion evoking video. Indeed these images were campaign images, but it was not an election campaign but rather a campaign to bring a brutal war criminal, child rapist, and murderer to justice. Both the textual information and the emotion evoking video requested that the readers and audience share the images, websites, and videos. It also requested that people contact the policy makers and leaders of pop culture listed on the site and ask them to help bring this man to justice.   Whether one agrees with how this website proposes to do this, one has to admit that Joseph Koney as well as the organization known as "Invisible Children" is now known by millions of people. KONY 2012's campaign worked because it brought out emotion and the campaigned channeled that emotion into action. Whether Kony is caught and at what price in human lives and suffering remains to be seen, but he is now known, and that is one of the main goals of the campaign.

Amazon

Amazon is a great place to sell independently produced DVD's, CD's, books, and the electronic or down-loadable versions of the same.   This site is a good way for independent musicians, movie makers, and authors to get their work onto the market place. This is due to the fact that Amazon is a well known site, and it also handles the payments processing. Amazon also allows authors, musicians, and movie makers to create profile to tell people a little about themselves. One of the good things about Amazon is the fact that one does not have to pay to be listed, and authors can earn a 70% royalty on works sold through Amazon. Amazon allows authors, musicians, and video makers to sell their works in either CD, CVD, book, or in electronic formats.

Information on paperback, CD, and DVD production and publishing can be found at http://www.createspace.com. Information on publishing electronic editions of books can be found at http://kdp.amazon.com. Information on publishing videos can be found at https://www.createspace.com/Products/VideoDownload/Index.jsp. Information of creating digital downloads for music can be found at https://www.createspace.com/Musician.jsp.

Flea Markets

Flea markets are another way to sell items. Flea markets are usually held on the weekends, but sometimes, they are also held on the weekdays. Flea markets are interesting due to the fact that there are usually many different variety of items offered for sale. Another way they are unique is that most vendors are every day people who supplement their weekday earnings. Some even sell at flea markets to earn their lively hood. A producer or publisher may not even have to set up their own table. They may sell a couple of items for the producer or publisher for a cut of the sales. It is a worthwhile effort to strike up a friendship with some of the vendors and offer them an opportunity to make a few more bucks on a consignment basis. People who have multiple items to sell may want to consider purchasing a space and sell directly to the public. Before doing such, one should contact the flea market management to determine rules, pricing, and any deadlines for purchasing tables for the specific time slot. Flea market locations can be found by searching the web for city, state, and "flea market." Websites specializing in flea market listings include http://www.fleamouse.com and http://www.fleaportal.com.

Trade Shows

Another place to sell and promote items is at
trade show. This venue is good is cases
where the content matches the purpose of the
trade show. Examples of this include selling
computer repair "how to" videos at a
computer show, or gun smithing books at gun
shows.   It is also a good place to learn new
information and meet possible competitors.

Special Events

In many different communities at many
different times of the year, special events are
held. These special events can range from
anything from charity fund-raisers, holiday
celebrations, tourist attraction events (Sturges
), to events celebrating a locality's history. In
any case, these special events are places
where people gather, and in many cases, these
events allow vendors to set up temporary
shop.

Product Placement

Another way to make money is to feature the

producer's or publisher's products and services that cater to the video's audience.

One way to do this is to place such a product in the scenery of a video or to include the product or service somehow in the programming. A how to video can feature an author's book if it is on a related subject or it can be used to advertise a more detailed DVD, CD, or video download.

Network Marketing

Many companies have set up thriving businesses by getting others to do the hard work for them. These companies use a technique called, "Network marketing" Network marketing involves having people sell items in order to keep some of the proceeds. People who brought the sellers into the program also make a small cut of the profit. Having family, friends, and acquaintances sell published and produced profits for a big cut of the profits, will allow the creator of the work plus friends and family share in the profits.

Unsolicited Electronic Advertisements - Spam

One reason why we are bombarded with a bunch of annoying crap in our email in-boxes is due to the fact that spamming is profitable even though it is unethical and in many cases, illegal. It is profitable because even though it costs recipients time to process and delete it, it costs very little in most cases to send it. Most people choose to ignore and delete it while others will actually purchase items advertised by spam. Other people, usually referred to by spammers as anti's will actually trace the origins of the spam and complain to the spammer's Internet provider as well as other services about the spamming. This usually results in the spammer getting his or her Internet account shut down or the spammer's account banned from the service on which the spam was sent. The author of this book is an "anti." The author of this book also knows the frustration of creating a product, promoting it on-line, and still receiving very few sales. However, the author still has not resorted to spamming and he will continue to create and promote products until one catches on in a big way.

Chapter 9
Where to Learn More

The purpose of this book is to get the reader started in production and publishing. It is intended to point the layperson in the right direction when it comes to low cost and free distribution of media.

If this book were to cover how to use each program listed within or every nuance of dealing with printing services, web hosting providers, or music and video websites, it would have to be as thick as several sets of encyclopedia's. It would be cost prohibitive to produce and publish such a tome, and the reader would probably not want to pay the cost of the resulting product.

However, the author of this book does not want to leave the reader wondering what to do next. This chapter provides much of that information. It is intended to provide information so that the reader will know where to go on-line to learn how to use specific programs listed in this book as well as how to find out even more information using search sites.

How to Use a Search Engine

A search engine is usually operated by a website. Such websites include http://www.ask.com, http://www.bing.com, http://www.google.com, http://www.yahoo.com, as well as many others. These websites allow people to type in what they are looking for, click on a search button, and viola, result appear. The problem with using search engines is that fact that many results point users to webpages that are irrelevant, want the user to shell out money for the information, or worse yet, try to install malicious software on the user's computer.

In order to separate the good results from the bad, there are several things that can be done. One is to put the search query in between quotation marks. For example, if one is searching for tutorials on how to use the application, Handbrake, he or she should use terms similar to "Handbrake tutorial" or something such as "How to use Handbrake."

If one searches these terms without using quotes, he or she is likely to receive results that may have only one of the words in it. In other words, the search engine may display sites that have the only the word "how" or only the word, Handbrake. This results listed may show information related to automobiles as these have hand brakes in them as well.

Another thing that should be taken into account for safety reasons is the reputation of the web sites shown in the search results. If the results show a You Tube page, or a page on sourceforge.net, then it is very likely to be safe. If the site is a part of lifehacker.com, it too is very likely safe. In fact, most tutorial websites are very likely to be safe. Those which prompt users to download anything such as a plug in, Active X object, codec, etc. should be looked upon with suspicion.

This chapter provides information not only on tutorials for the software discussed in this book, but it also provides places on where to learn techniques for recording video, audio, and techniques for formatting and publishing book. Also included is information on where to learn website authoring.

Website Authoring and Language Tutorials

This book lists more than one resource in the even a website is taken off-line or otherwise discontinued. More information about learning HTML, CSS, Javascript, Java, etc can be found at these sites listed below:

http://www.w3schools.com/ is one of the most valuable free to use.

Another site for rank beginners is http://www.pagetutor.com/html_tutor/index.html.

Also deserving mention is http://www.w3.org/MarkUp/Guide/.

http://www.youtube.com/watch?v=v4oN4DuR7YU is a video tutorial on HTML design.

http://www.youtube.com/watch?v=Wz2klMXDqF4 is a video on CSS design.

Tutorials on Uploading

There are many different ways of uploading or publishing information   to a hosting service.   These include both web based uploading and FTP (file Transfer Protocol) uploading.   Site may support one or both depending on the hosting provider. Where to find more information and tutorials can be found in this section.

A tutorial for the File Transfer Protocol are listed below:

http://www.freewebmasterhelp.com/tutorials/ftp

http://www.phpjunkyard.com/tutorials/ftp-chmod-tutorial.php

http://www.mediacollege.com/internet/ftp/

Some video tutorials can also be found.

http://www.youtube.com/watch?v=O3DudpEMPiY show how to do it with Filezilla, but other programs operate in a similar fashion.

http://www.ntchosting.com/videos/how-to-upload-files-with-ftp-client.html is another one using Filezilla.

Audio and Video Acquisition

This book covered some very basic techniques and method of acquiring audio and visual content. However, there is much more to be learned. Fortunately, there are websites that teach how to do these things for free. It needs to be stressed that reading the equipment manual is of paramount importance.. This manual can be usually obtained on-line if it is not kept with the camera itself.

One important website is http://www.mediacollege.com/. This site is highly recommended by the author.

Another site that provides good information is http://lifehacker.com/214043/8-ways-to-shoot-video-like-a-pro.

DVD Authoring

DVD Authoring allows video to be converted to a format that just about every DVD player should play. There first few links discuss DVD authoring in general, and the rest of the segment lists places to learn how to use the specific programs discussed in this book.

Tutorials explaining the process can be found below:

http://www.transcoding.org/transcode?
Tutorials/Authoring_PC_Media_To_DVD
is a relatively complicated explanation of the process.

http://www.tappin.me.uk/Linux/dvd.html
is a somewhat easier to understand lesson.

http://www.recipester.org/Topics/DVD_Au
thoring provides some more insightful information on DVD authoring

Bombono

One easy to use tutorial can be found at

http://www.bombono.org/cgi-bin/wiki/Bombono_Tutorial .

Another can be found at http://www.my-guides.net/en/guides/linux-dvd-video/214-how-to-author-a-dvd-using-bombono-dvd.

http://www.youtube.com/watch?v=mCG2B9a7TOE show a video tutorial on how to use Bombono.

DVD Styler

http://www.dvdstyler.org/en/?option=com_content&view=article&id=70&Itemid=53&lang=en is a tutorial from the DVD Styler creator's site.

http://www.aimersoft.com/how-to-burn/dvdstyler-tutorial.html is another tutorial.

To watch a video tutorial, go to http://www.youtube.com/watch?v=TVTSWvz1eCQ

http://www.youtube.com/watch?v=VCvMWGdVqHI is another video.

DVD Flick

DVD Flick has many different feature that may take some time to learn. It is best to view the tutorials listed in this section in order to get a hang of how to use the program.

One textual tutorial available for free download can be found at http://www.dvdflick.net/guide.php.

http://www.youtube.com/watch?v=u2qDK_z2bYI is a video tutorial on how to use DVD Flick.

http://www.youtube.com/watch?v=V5DpzyQ4lvw is a video on how to customize DVD menu templates.

http://www.youtube.com/watch?v=gHBlVbEYSM0 is yet another tutorial on how to use the program.

CD and DVD Burning Programs

This section includes tutorials on the CD and DVD writing programs presented in this book.

Infrarecorder

http://infrarecorder.org/?page_id=27 is a set of tutorials made by the creators of the program.

http://gofree.com/Tutorials/InfraRecorder TutorialDataCD.php is another textual tutorial.

http://showmedo.com/videotutorials/video? name=1090030&fromSeriesID=109 is where one can find a decent video tutorial.

CDBurner XP

http://www.aimersoft.com/how-to-burn/cdburnerxp-tutorial.html is a rudimentary guide to using CDBurner XP.

http://www.youtube.com/watch? v=3qwHAd6ZIh8&feature=related is a video tutorial for the program.

K3B

http://tutorial.downloadatoz.com/k3b.html is a very basic textual tutorial on how to use K3B.

http://ubuntuforums.org/showthread.php?t=218165 is another textual tutorial that covers more topics

Screen Recording Programs

This section provides information on where to find tutorials for using the programs that record what is happening on a computer's monitor.

Camstudio

http://www.scribd.com/doc/13328453/CamStudio-Tutorial is a good text tutorial on how to use this program.

http://www.youtube.com/watch?v=Kiug3H3c4gk is a good video tutorial on this program.

RecordMyDesktop

http://www.linuxplanet.com/linuxplanet/tu torials/6489/1 is a good textual tutorial.

http://www.youtube.com/watch?v=gTN-jaHqpds is a video tutorial.

Quicktime

http://cksolutions.ie/record-screen-mac-os-quicktime/ is a textual tutorial on how to do screen recording.

http://macmost.com/quicktime-x-screen-recording.html is a good video tutorial on how to use Quicktime for recording screens.

Audio Processing Programs

The audio programs presented in this book are generally very easy to use. However, some who have never used audio editing programs may want instructions. Some of the video processing programs listed in the next part of this chapter also include audio processing capabilities.

Alis

Tutorials for the Alis recording program are sketchy and hard to come by, but a few screen shots are available at http://sourceforge.net/projects/alis/.

Audacity

Audacity is very popular and comes with many different tutorials One textual tutorial can be found by visiting http://audacity.sourceforge.net/manual-1.2/tutorials.html.

Another good tutorial can be found by visiting http://www.lifelonglearner.us/other/audacity/.

A good video tutorial for Audacity can be found at http://www.youtube.com/watch?v=lrPGMjZORCM.

Sox

One good tutorial on how to use Sox can be

found at
http://www.thegeekstuff.com/2009/05/soun
d-exchange-sox-15-examples-to-
manipulate-audio-files/.

Another can be found at
http://billposer.org/Linguistics/Computatio
n/SoxTutorial.html.

Video Processing Programs

There are several video processing programs
listed here. Each has different capabilities
and effects. It is possible to use a
combination of these programs to put together
powerful videos.

Avidemux

A good textual tutorial with screenshots can
be found at
http://en.flossmanuals.net/avidemux/.

Another textual tutorial can be found at
http://dramatizables.tolewis.info/1a813fa8e
ee45b0a6d4e10c2d5/C/xwomB1/fr/vy42384.
j6/04eb.

A video tutorial can be found at
http://www.youtube.com/watch?
v=X23I2BZ4J5A

Handbrake

A decent video tutorial can be found by
visiting
http://www.metacafe.com/watch/8289836/h
andbrake_tutorial/.

A pdf file that has good information about
using Handbrake can be found at
http://www.moorecast.com/upload_user/H
andbrake_Tutorial.pdf.

http://www.youtube.com/watch?
v=x88xM4vl0zk is another video tutorial.

Cinelerra

The makers of Cinelerra provide an on-line
textual tutorial available at
http://heroinewarrior.com/cinelerra/cineler
ra.html. This tutorial runs the gamut from
installation to how to use effects and
transitions.

http://www.youtube.com/watch?
v=X23I2BZ4J5A is a decent video on how to
use this software.

http://www.youtube.com/watch?
v=hpITa27K-6o is a very good, multi-part
tutorial on how to use this powerful software.

iMovie

Apple Computer has a good tutorial for their
product, iMovie. It is available by visiting
http://www.apple.com/support/imovie/.

A downloadable manual on how to use
iMovie is available at
http://manuals.info.apple.com/en/iMovie_0
8_Getting_Started.pdf.

Here is a simple video tutorial on iMovie –
http://www.youtube.com/watch?v=5YbA-
g1meCg.

Another basic video tutorial can be found at
http://www.youtube.com/watch?
v=aEJjvhnA1wQ.

Kdenlive

http://www.kdenlive.org/tutorial is a set of video tutorials available from the creators of the application themselves.

Another tutorial put out by Wikibooks is located at http://en.wikibooks.org/wiki/Kdenlive/Quickstart

One can find a list of several video tutorials for different Kdenlive by going to http://www.youtube.com/playlist?list=PL687F9B71B35BFFCE

Windows Movie Maker

To see Microsoft's instructions on Windows Movie Maker, visit http://windows.microsoft.com/en-US/windows-vista/Getting-started-with-Windows-Movie-Maker

Another screen shot based tutorial can be found at

http://www.slideshare.net/macloo/windows
-movie-maker-tutorial.

One last textual tutorial can be found at
http://presentationsoft.about.com/od/movie
maker/a/mov_mak_beg.htm.

VideoLAN Movie Creator

Since VideoLAN Movie Creator is a
relatively new application still under
development, there are not too many tutorials
available for it yet.

One can find screen shots by visiting
http://trac.videolan.org/vlmc/wiki/Screensh
ots.

A video tutorial can be found by going to
http://www.youtube.com/watch?
v=DQjxt01d43g.

Virtualdub

The makers of Virtualdub created a tutorial
that can be found at
http://www.virtualdub.org/virtualdub_doc
s.html.

A pdf tutorial can be downloaded by visiting http://digilander.libero.it/fotografarte/DO_ NOT_DELETE/VirtualDub_tutorial.pdf.

A video tutorial for Virtualdub can be found at http://www.youtube.com/watch? v=JjWwlaE8kps.

Wax

There is a video tutorial about Wax that is available from its creators. It can be accessed by visiting http://www.debugmode.com/tuts/wax/first use.htm.

Another textual tutorial can be found at http://www.instructables.com/id/Wax-20-tutorial/.

A video tutorial for Wax can be found at http://www.5min.com/Video/Advanced-WAX-20-Tutorial-97931787,

Another video tutorial can be found at http://www.youtube.com/watch? v=cxlDTJgpZ58.

A brief tutorial summarizing the effects available with Wax can be found at http://www.youtube.com/watch? v=RRgjI71T42E.

ZS4

A video tutorial for ZS4 can be found at http://www.youtube.com/watch? v=xwEEF8mB0sk.

Another video tutorial can be found at http://zomobo.net/zs4-tutorial.

How to Use Ripping, and Downloading Programs

This section provides information on how to use download and ripping programs to extract video and audio from media on-line and in CD or DVD formats.

DVDx

One good, user edited, textual tutorial for using DVDx can be found by visiting http://www.wikihow.com/Rip-a-DVD-to-an-AVI-or-MPG-File-Using-DVDx.

A good video tutorial can be found at http://www.softoxi.com/dvdx-video-trailer-screenshots.html.

A good list of links providing tutorials on how to perform specific tasks can be found at A good video tutorial can be found at http://www.labdv.com/dvdx/help.php.

A good video tutorial can be found at http://www.softoxi.com/dvdx-video-trailer-screenshots.html

DVD Shrink

A textual tutorial for using DVD Shrink can be found by visiting http://www.ehow.com/facts_4827139_dvd-shrink-tutorial.html.

A decent video tutorial can be found at http://www.youtube.com/watch?v=tdBsYgBILrw. DVD Shrink is a relatively simple program to use.

Download Helper

http://www.downloadhelper.net/tutorials.php is a webpage with a list of how to do many tasks using the Download Helper Firefox extension.

A video tutorial can be found by visiting http://www.youtube.com/watch?v=VGF_BJk6Gb0.

Vuze

http://www.fanhow.com/Software/Vuze provides a list of articles on how to use the Vuze bittorrent client.

One can learn how to use the ever popular magnet protocol to download files with Vuze. A web page for using magnet links can be found by visiting http://wiki.vuze.com/w/Magnet_link.

How to Use Book Publishing Programs

Learning how to use free programs to create books does take a bit of time, but the monetary savings are worth it. This section shows different packages and how they can be each used. http://www.techsupportalert.com/best-free-desktop-publishing-program.htm is one webpage that discusses some free programs.

Another page that discusses free desktop publishing software can be found by visiting http://desktoppub.about.com/od/findsoftware1/tp/freedtpsoftware.htm.

Sigil

Google code has a textual tutorial on how to use Sigil. It is located at http://code.google.com/p/sigil/wiki/BasicTutorial.

Another good tutorial can be found by visiting http://www.passwordincorrect.com/2011/10/07/creating-epub-ebooks-with-sigil-1-getting-started/.

Calibre

A good textual tutorial can be found by visiting http://manual.calibre-ebook.com/.

A decent video demonstration of Calibre can be found by visiting http://calibre-ebook.com/demo.

Open Office

An excellent textual tutorial on how to use Open Office for book publishing can be found by visiting http://maketecheasier.com/layout-a-book-with-openoffice-org-part-1/2009/07/13

An excellent video tutorial for page layout and design for using Open Office for books can be found at http://www.youtube.com/watch?v=Dsej93edn4w.

The Internet is full of resources and tutorials for learning publishing and production as well as the software discussed in this book.

Glossary

authoring - the process of creating a work, the process of creating a DVD or CD that is playable by most or all players.

Bar code - A graphic image designed specifically to provide information to be read by machines.

Cascading style sheet (CSS) - file or files used to enhance the display of content in a web browser

downloading - the process of receiving a file from another computer, phone or other device

domain name - the name of a computer that is typed in in order access that computer - an identification string that defines a realm of administrative autonomy, authority, or control on the Internet such as freelink.cx, google.com, etc.

domain registrar - a company that allows people to purchase the use of a domain name for a period of time editing - the process of changing a file to add content, delete content, or correct errors

effects - a modification designed to change or enhance the display or sound of multimedia files.

host - a computer connected to an computer network such as the Internet.

hosting provider - a company that provides computing or servers that are connected to the Internet

HTML - Hypertext Markup Language - a language used to instruct web browsers on how to display content.

International Standard Book Number (ISBN) - an unique nine or thirteen digit number assigned individually to each commercially published book

International Standard Serial Number (ISSN) - an unique number assigned to published periodical material

Java - a programming language designed so that its object code works on many different platforms and devices.

Javascript – an interpreted scripting language that is used in web design as well as other applications

loop – a short clip of audio or video designed to be repeatedly played that is used for background purposes such as a DVD menu

media player - a device or software used to play back multimedia files such as audio or video files.

ripping - the process of extracting audio or video from a CD, DVD, or other content

registrar - a company that allows people to purchase the use of a domain name for a period of time

server – a computer or computer program that is used to serve request of other computers or computer programs.

streaming – the act of playing a video or audio file as it is being transmitted from a site

template – a pattern that facilitates design or construction such as a web site template or a DVD design template.

transcoding - the process of converting a file from one format to another – usually used to describe the conversion of sound or video files

uploading - the process of sending a file to another computer, phone, or other device

web browser - software used to display web pages such as Chrome, Firefox, Internet Explorer, Safari, etc.

webpage - an individual page on a site that can be viewed without having to click on a link.

web site – a collection of webpages, files, etc that is hosted under a domain name

Index

A

Alis 37, 159
Amazon 12, 19-23, 91, 118, 120, 140-141
Audacity 38-39, 42, 45, 48, 159
authoring 75-78, 81, 149-150, 153, 170
Avidemux 40, 42, 160

B

bar code 83, 131-132, 134-136, 171
Barnes and Noble 21, 91
Bombono 77-78, 153-154

C

Cafe Press 21-22
Calibre 92, 170
camcorder 33, 35-37, 42, 54, 56-58, 65
camera(s) 54-61, 79, 136, 152
Camstudio 79, 157
CDBurner XP 48, 156
cellphone(s) 54, 59-60, 80, 117
Cinelerra 67-68, 161
Chrome 174
clandestine devices 60

Create Space 12, 22-23, 26, 84-85, 118, 132, 136

D

Disc Makers 24
Download Helper 44, 62, 168
DVD Shrink 64, 167
DVDFlick 78, 155
DVDStyler 78, 154
DVDx 64, 166

E

effects 66-69, 71, 87, 102, 160-161, 166, 172
extract(ed)(ion) 33, 36-38, 39-42, 166, 173

F

Ffmpeg 74-75
Firefox 44, 62-63, 122, 168, 174
flea market(s) 141-142

G

GIMP 84-85, 87
GOCR 95

H

Handbrake 42-43, 75, 148-149, 161
HTML 85, 88, 93, 98, 101-106, 150, 172
Hypertext Markup Language 101, 172

I

Infrarecorder 47-48, 156
iMovie 68, 162
iPad 61, 113
International Standard Book Number 22, 83, 134, 172
International Standard Serial Number 135, 172
ISBN 17, 22, 24, 83, 132, 134-136, 172
ISSN 135, 136, 172

J

Java 37, 103-104, 136, 150, 173
Javascript 101-103, 150, 173

K

K3B 49, 157

Kdenlive 68-69, 163
Kindle 12-13, 19-20, 91

L

Lightning Press 23
Lulu 23, 26
lxDVDRip 64-65

M

Metacafe 62, 115
MySpaceTV 115

N

network marketing 144
Nook 21, 91

O

OCR 94-95
Openbexi 105
Open Office 84-87, 106, 170
Optical Character Recognition 94-95

P

paperback 9, 12-13, 22, 83, 129, 141
product placement 143

Q

Quicktime 79, 158

R

RecordMyDesktop 79, 158
ripping 54, 63-64, 166, 173
Roku 11, 53, 113-114, 116

S

Sigil 93, 169
Smashwords 24
Sox 43, 159

T

tablet computer(s) 54, 61, 96, 131
TesseractOCR 95

U

Universal Product Code 22, 133
UPC 17, 22, 24, 120, 132-134, 136

V

VideoLAN Movie Creator 70, 73, 164
Virtualdub 71, 164-165
Vuze 63, 168

W

Wax 71, 165-166
webcam(s) 59
webpage(s) 97-99, 101-105, 117, 148, 168-169, 174
Windows Movie Maker 69, 163

X

XHTML 98

Y

You Tube 36, 39, 62, 101, 114, 117, 121, 123, 149

Z

www.ingramcontent.com/pod-product-compliance
Lightning Source LLC
Chambersburg PA
CBHW071148050326
40689CB00011B/2022